For Candy

But how could anyone, much less a girl,
withstand the will of Jove? . . .
Ovid
The Metamorphoses
Book III, "Jove and the
Arcadian Nymph"

Already I fear he may so sore have erred
That I have risen to succor him too late,
From what of him in Heaven I have heard
Dante
The Divine Comedy
"Inferno"
Canto II, lines 64-66

Earth would have been too much - I see -
And Heaven - not enough for me -
Emily Dickinson
Collected Poems
No. 313

Love is itself unmoving,
Only the cause and end of movement,
T.S. Eliot
"Burnt Norton"

01

A Pause in the Kinesis.

Red.

Loose walking shorts. The elastic is shot in the right leg-hole of her panties. She is talking to her companion. She seems unaware of my intrusion. I will remain unobtrusive. Wait for her leg to tire.

Patience is not my strong suit. Nor do I do well with inactivity.

A test.

I take a deep breath, blow air across the surface of my coffee, watch the passersby on the street beyond the window.

The shoulderbags or briefcases with suits attached pendulum by. The schoolkids amble along with their knapsacks of books and lunches and sidearms concealed here or tucked snugly against their hips or in their armpits. The electrical utility repair crew plays with wires down the open cylinder while the *paving man leans on his two-handed rammer, the reporter's lead flies swiftly over the note-book, the sign-painter is lettering with blue and gold*[1]. *. . some who keep the Sabbath going to Church . . . or in Surplice*[2] *. . .* and, scattered throughout, *the dead alive*[3] and *their high-born kinsmen*[4] . . .

I scribble on a napkin, blow breath, drink coffee.

After a century or more, cups are drained and they prepare to rise. Her friend rises first. Blocks my view.

Elohi, Elohi, lama shebaqtani?[5]

I can only imagine the brown-red hair. The glorious crease.

The moment is lost. Movement resumes.

1

I rise and follow. They divide. I follow her into a
bank branch, conceal myself behind a potted ficus. While I
study the new rates for installment loans, home equity
loans, mortgages, she fills out a deposit slip and envelope,
drops it into the quick-deposit box. Heads for the door. As
she passes, her step stutters, her eyes flicker a moment,
then lock. She gives me a hard look. Very hard.

*If you are behind me on the street, I will turn and
kill you.*

I consider it for a moment. She spins swiftly
through the exit. I put a person between she and me, re-
volve through the door, then recede back into my world.

At my desk, I remove shrink-wrap from my book-
without- words and begin to scrawl.

I found it behind a cobweb
in a lock box in my mind,
hidden by the potted plant of a banking transaction.
There was only the one, long-forgotten item,
but I knew it would fit
and it still had her smell,
although
I'd never experienced the odor before
and more than likely never will again,
but
I'd know it anywhere,
anytime,
even though I'd quite forgotten it.

I tried the fit of the red wool slipper,
if only in my mind,
luxuriated in its warmth,
inhaled the must of its retentive humidity.
As a concept, it now seemed distant

2

from its origin --
laundry chute for Heaven's unwashed --
more now a haven against security,
the retainer of explosions, muffled
and hid from common view.

An armstroke broke my reverie,
a blink and it was gone.
Then she finished writing what she wrote
and disappeared around the revolving door.

I call it "The Red Wool Slipper." I don't always title
my poems, but this title . . . fits . . . nicely.

02

It is as if I have awakened from a blow to the head, with little -- no, with no -- idea of who I am, where I am, or what I am doing here. I am returning from an evening in a fleabag motel with Ruth, the otherwise wife of my next-door neighbor. Short-stay, fuck motel. Mirrors on the ceiling. Roaches in the john. It has been incredible. Not that Ruth is anything special. It is the excitement of knowing she is married to the jerk who lives next door, Walter, and that he'd kill me if he found out.

We left by separate doors, separate cars.

But now, I pull off to the side of the road and scream. I am screaming my brains out, literally. But my voice is trapped inside the shatter-proof glass, a pantomime of expanding pressure until my head explodes, splattering the inside of my relic Datsun 280Z with blood and brains and skull fragments.

Gloria.

The smell of Ruth hangs heavy in the air, emitted from my sweaty, headless chest.

Gloria?

Someone is trying to mind-meld with me.

I reassemble the pieces. I have to.

I don't *know* anyone named Gloria. Perhaps the words to the popular song. What popular song? Van Morrison. The '70s. No. The word to the chant. The ancient one. The only one. Is that it?

My vision is trying to reestablish itself. My focus is uncertain, unclear.

The chariot tears across the windshield, rolls into a ball of fire, then accelerates down the road before me. Or

4

is the ball of fire me? Or am I it? For I am sucked into its wake, to the whip, cherub-borne, to victory. To glory. *Gloria*. What is going on here? I do not know. I cannot tell. I have no reason why. That face. I've seen that face before. ... *his fierce Chariot roll'd, as with the sound of torrent Floods[1]*. Was that face mine, or that of an impostor, a pretender to the throne? A replacement? God, no.

I drive home for dinner with Oomieka and the kids. But I am late. What was I thinking? I am very late. As usual. She does not expect me, for I am seldom home before late. They have eaten, of course, hours before, but I do not care. Food no longer nourishes me. Only poetry.

Green Cheese.

"I was once your poem," she has said.

She was.

"The children?" I ask, although I cannot think of why.

"Upstairs. Homework. And TV, of course."

Fifty and I still have children at home. We had them late. Oomieka needed to finish med school. One of us would have to earn a decent living. Teaching wouldn't do it. Teaching English, Funglus.[2] I am a teacher with nothing to teach to no one ... double negative ... and more ... or less. No, none, nothing. Less? What is less than nothing. The thing is I think I know. Know? Is that no, again?

"You look a bit out of sorts," she says, "I mean even for you."

"Hey, you would, too, if you had been sucked into a fireball shortly after your head had exploded and you had barely reassembled the pieces."

"Another headache?"

"No."

"The fiorinal with codeine is where you left it."

5

"Where?"

"In your office. Your inner sanctum. Your . . . package."

"Oomieka?"

"No," she cuts me off. "I know how you are when you are in this phase. *You* work it out, then we can speak again."

"It constipates me, the fiorinal with codeine."

She shakes her head.

Phase? My *life* is a phase. A phrase. An incomplete statement. Half-assed, etc. . . . Oh, what the fuck.

She is back to her needlepoint. It relaxes her hands, un-stresses her fingers. Those magical digits that return life to those who would otherwise abandon it. It seems simple justice that life should be restored by a being so beautiful. What did she ever see in me . . . who is so unlike she? She has her shit together, understands mathematics, the laws of motion, how the cardio-vascular system keeps pumping, where to put the knife. I . . . can't stand the sight of blood, or anything red. But red was the color of the guidons raised for my greatest victory . . . This detachment from reality is getting worrisome, sometimes even for me. In the past it's been my source of relaxation, was done with levity. Now . . . "my greatest victory?" What the fuck is going on here?

"Go upstairs and write," she says. "It's what you need to do to get yourself through this."

Through this? Ah, Oomieka, things are so easy for you. Life is so easy for you. All the answers simple, empirical. Oomieka. With the almost-almond eyes and the not-quite-epicanthic lids. It doesn't matter, one way or the other. She never closes her eyes anyway. I have never met anyone so aware. So aware of earth and unaware of air. Strange. Definitely not hereditary. Her mother was a con-

6

cert-grade violinist. A pre-Suzuki, Suzuki. Her father . . . she never speaks of him, never spoke of him. But some evidence cannot be overlooked. White. He must have been white. A scientist, I've long supposed. One of those who made the bomb. The man who provided Armageddon for the parents of her mom. Hell, they were old anyway. That's for sure. They were about my age.

I turn and mount the stair.[3]

Sarah and Amanda are ensconced in their rooms, at their desks with their televisions going . . . going, gone. I imagine myself kicking in the tubes. I feel no attachment to my children. They were the results of two glorious fucks, little more. God, she was beautiful. I couldn't keep my hands off her, my dick in my pants. Shit, that night in Cap d'Antibes. There'd be three, if we. . .

I miss her. I miss her terribly. Will we be alone in the end?

To prevent a recurrence, she had a tubal ligation when she was thirty-five. I won't go through that again, she said at the time. What? Go through what?

I enter my den. In the semi-dark, I negotiate the columns of papers, books and magazines stacked randomly about. I sit, switch on the desklamp. Its rays reflect off the surface of my desk, streaked in a thin layer of dust. I don't have time to tidy. I have things to do, I can't fuck around with ordinary shit. I swing my legs onto the corner of the desk, take up my notebook and my fountain pen and gaze into the lamp.

Green Cheese.

My reason for living. Now, my only reason for living. The rage is building again. It is the scream suppressed. My brain is in strain, agaayn (in the plaayn?). It needs to blow. I take up my pen to write. Scribble some thoughts about the experience in the car. . .

7

My 280Z did two flips on the parkway
and came to rest upside down
alongside a deciduous tree in foliage season.
I'd missed my turn. . . .
Something is tugging me away from this. I can't get
a fix. Resume writing . . .
I was a bit shaken but otherwise OK.
My skull had been crushed like an eggshell
but, what the hell,
I didn't think it would last forever.
The shards of Plexiglas from the shattered T-roof
embedded in my brain were a bit of an annoyance
but life, as they say, goes on. . . .
It's there again, the pull. I try to focus, cannot.
Scratch on . . .
The wheels of the inverted Z continued to spin
like the hands of a clock.
I watched them for a while, but you know how hard
it is
to pick up the motion of clock hands. . . .
There is no time.
?
I put down my pen. Become acutely aware of the
buzz.
A fly alights upon my stapler, drawn to it by the re-
flection of my desk lamp in its chrome-plated crown. I
swipe my open palm through the air a fraction of an inch
above the fly. Alerted by the draft to the fast-approaching
danger, he takes off, but I sweep him into my closing fingers. I pause a moment to feel him buzzing in the hollow
of my hand. I shake my hand violently to numb him, then
slam his body into the wall above my wastepaper basket.

8

His body falls lifeless into the can. Two points. Yes! I have perfected this maneuver, all of it, from the swipe to the slam-dunk of the dead fly. It allows me to kill without dirtying my hands.

My head is feeling a little better, but the blood has left the lower leg. I recross it on top of the other. The agitated dust glistens in the lamplight. It swirls. Begins to take shape. I begin to scratch with the ancient pen, again. I love the sound it makes, the way the ink flows too freely, sometimes stains my fingers . . . flowing as if by its own volition . . .

She stands in the room
                    now
the office where I am writing with my feet on the corner of the desk
            where I pen, now, the syllables
Glor-i-ya. (nice touch, the thing with the hyphens and the y . . . why?)
            I'm stuck, watch the dust swirl, begin again
She says . . . ?
            I can't get a grip on it.
"I am . . .
I am death," she says. . . *That's not it, but it'll fill the space*
for now.
with the light of the sun where her face should have been.

When she smiles, she does not have the lines at the corners of her eyes.
I thought I saw them for an instant,
                    then
they were absorbed back
beneath the surface of

9

her skin.
Glor-i-ya.
Mind-melding,
again.
Then.
She is gone.
She is just toying with me.
This time.

I like it. Oomieka is right. Writing will get me through it.

03

"I am your connection."
She has descended into the chair.
The face.
Remembrance of things past.
Future.
Now.
She sits there in a '60s dress, her legs spread and the slack in the abundant cloth forming a bowl-like indentation between her thighs. I half expect her to start shucking peas. She is a girl of twenty, perhaps twenty-one.
"Meaning?" I ask.
"I have no *meaning*."
"Ah, an intellectual exercise," I say threading my fingers into the cat's cradle. "Those are always fun."
"Quite the contrary."
"Meanin--... Sorry. I forgot. You are meaningless."
"That's not what I said."
"But it is what you meh-an-tt. Uh-oh. Did it again."
She smiles. It is more a wrinkle gathering along her lip-line like the tightening of a draw-string bag, or a cunt at rest. She is quite attractive, from my perspective, for what it's worth. Skin the color of chalk, laced in thin threads of blue; hair long, long strings of twisted black. The thin delicate nose, an uninterrupted line. She has the smell about her. Hers is familiar, although a distant memory. A dash of light sparks across her irises, from left to right. It is a fright. I need to recoil but cannot, this time. *Noli me tangere.*[1] A pity.

The scent.

The fragrant oil.

"Are you wearing perfume?"

"No."

"What is that smell? I find it very pleasant."

"The scent is me."

"I see."

"You seem to have your senses confused."

I study her a moment. I don't know if we are still in the midst of games.

"Do we exchange names?" I venture, suddenly acutely aware of nothing but the smell and wondering all of a sudden about this "connection" thing. Connection. As in erection?

"Altagloria," she says folding her hands and dropping them into that peasant's lap.

"Like the words of the popular song."

"What song?"

"Never mind. Say, shouldn't it be Alta*gracia*?"

"My mother got it wrong."

"Of course, the child is mother to the mother."

"None other."

"Do you always speak in rhymes?"

"Not always . . . just sometimes."

"Stop it!" I snap.

"OK. No need to cause a flap."

How the fuck did she do that?

"Just call me Alley, like the cat."

She bats her long black lashes.

I am afraid to move. Snap/flap; that/cat. What now, pray tell?

"I double the A not the L."

"Of course."

"And you?"

12

"I'm Max, as in maximum, or Maximillian, in which case I double the L."

"Like hell."

"Well . . . yes."

With that I fizzle. The words run out. We sit in silence for a while, then I unwind my fingers, bloodless and numb now, and begin drumming them on the desk.

"Yes, of course," she says into the void, "the wherefore and the why. I was sitting beneath a tree on the quadrangle just now and you went walking by."

"I've been here for thirteen years."

"And I for less than one . . . "

Is that zero?

". . . day."

She stops at that. And sits. As if I have broken her chain of thoughts, and they are now scattered in uncoded directions, difficult to retrieve. In my head the scream grows in the distance now. It is highly pitched and barely audible, and beginning to pain.

"I came as soon as I knew," she resumes, finally.

"Knew what?"

"That I was your connection."

"But you said you only saw me for the first time a few minutes ago."

"Time has no meaning."

"Nor does meaning; we've already established that."

"Exactly."

"This *is* getting to be fun."

"You've killed," she says, from nowhere.

"What are you talking about?"

"You've stolen and you've killed . . . and more."

The blood drains from my brain. The scream goes muffled.

13

"You've been influenced, a greater crime, but I'm not sure by whom."

"The verse is sometimes free, I see," I say to break this new tension.

"Hey," she says, now, "that's me. But hardly worth a mention."

She is at it again. I say, "I don't know which is worse, rhymed couplets or free verse."

"My curse."

"Ah, shit."

"This time, you started it."

Suddenly, my eyes cannot endure hers. They are emerald green, with flecks of black that float kaleidoscopically when they should be staying put. I need an anchor not a raft. I roll mine back and gaze about the room. Oomieka is right. Rooms *have* become my packaging. And when I am packaged, I feel safe, secure. My office at the university means first that I have a job, gainful employment, a visible means of support. Second, it is where I hold forth, hold court, hold off . . .

But she is here now, Alta-Gloria, inside my package, taking the measure of me. Nah. She is beyond that.

"Does this mean we get to fuck?" I ask. *I'll take a rhyme to mean success.*

"Yes . . . of course."

Did that rhyme? How long must a rhyme exist to be a rhyme? There is no time.

"I said, 'yes.' The rhyme is redundant."

The skinless fingers of a desert palm scratch at the leaden pains behind my head, a reminder of my mortality, my former life, my former death. Get real. This is late November, up north, and the finger-nail screech is a snappable twig at the extremity of a deciduous, a toothpick for a harpy foraging for dead souls.

14

And as the late leaves of November fall
To earth, one after another, ever fewer,
Till the bough sees its spoil gone past recall . . .[2]
This morbidity of late, I hate. It's not me, but it has
taken hold of me.

"Well, shall we?" she says rising, ". . . go."

"If we must."

"Hey this fucking thing was your idea."

"I don't know . . . "

"Ain't that the truth."

"What?"

"You coming?" The glint in her eye is obscene; the
smile again a wrinkled vulva. She turns and leaves the
room.

"S . . . soon," I breathe.

I leave, two steps behind.

"I have an apartment off campus on Hill," she says,
as we pass beneath the ivied arch at the front of the admin
building. "We'll go by separate routes -- you have your rep
to think of."

"Think?"

She sighs. "Oh, never mind. Look, when you get
to Hill, you'll note the houses all alike. Walk on the south
side until you see me behind the glass door. When I see
you've seen me, I'll turn and mount the stairs -- I'm on the
third floor. You may come in then. The door will be ajar."
A port in air.[3]

"How far?" Suddenly I feel quite lame, a stitch
knifes through my side, as if I have run a marathon instead
of walking only a couple of blocks, after spending all day
pinned to my classes, nailed to my desk. Pinned and wriggling.[4]

She goes left. I . . . go right. It is as she commands. She is, after all, my connection.

15

I walk the grey stone streets. The page of an out-of-date newspaper tumbles along the curb and comes to rest in a sea of waste-water iced with a tiny oil slick. The jump head says something about the sorry state of education. Amen to that, brothers. Three limpid blades of grass, still green, are angry at being left out here to die. Hey, what can I say; I didn't do it . . . did I? I shiver in the chill. It makes me want to pee. My bladder is contracting, my prostate expanding inside me.

Ah, distinctly I remember,
this day in late November
when each dying ember,
this wastrel did implore.
Will it be warm . . .
and more?[5]
This poetry shit is fucking taking over.

It *is* a bleak day. It is one of those beautifully, terrifyingly, bleak days where blue skies are covered alternately with rim-lit clouds of grey to black, billows of smoke from a wrecked tanker, cold, black smoke that somehow, miraculously, unleashes squalls of pure, white snow. Go figure.

The poetry had taken over years before. It is anti-knowledge. Strings of words created to emote. But the music has always been in short, timpanic bursts. Where is the sustained measure I've been looking for?

Just words and nothing more.

The houses are all aligned, as she has said, in some other-day design: turn-of-the-century rowhouse, if you ask me, each with a half-dozen stone steps, framed in formidable stone balustrades, to a stone porch; great floor-to-ceiling windows to the right, beneath which are window boxes with quick-frozen geraniums now grey to match the weather; to the left a heavy, metal-and-glass door, behind

16

the third one down the street of which, back-lit in the tropical orange of an antique chandelier, stands the figure of Altagloria. Highest glory. Glory on high. Aaley, like the cat.
She turns and mounts the inner stair. I turn and
mount the outer. Will there be time to turn back and descend the stair? Time to replace the baldspot in the middle
of my hair?[6] Time to return from here to nowhere? There
is no time. Everywhere is nowhere.
   She pulls me into her place, then turns and bolts the
door. Radiators clank an attack against the evening chill.
The flat is wonderfully warm with the smell of steam-
heated paint, a memory of my childhood in elementary
school, those cold, dark weeks just after Christmas, when
the only pleasure in life was the smell of the hot paint on
the old radiators. My mother cooking dinner now drifts before my eyes. My father I don't remember, but my guess is
he was wise.
   Down a foyer, she leads me, to a room lit only by
spillage from the hall. She turns me to her, backs me up a
step, then kisses me with moistened lips. "Wait here," she
says and pushes me to a bed.
   "Where'm I going?"
   "We shall see." With a flick, she removes the outer
light, then disappears somewhere . . . nowhere.
   I remove my glasses and lay them on the night table. As my eyes adjust to the darkness, I see only abstrac-
tions. I close my lids and watch the molecular dance on
the inside. Limbs twisting, bodies falling through the grey-
black smoke of some militarily induced fire, to a world red-
dened by my vision. . . . *headlong they threw themselves
Down from the verge* . . . [7] The darkness rosies further and
the bodies disappear.
   The sound of a door opening awakens me. Disoriented, for an instant, I don't know where I am. Then, when

17

I get my bearings, I panic. I am naked, beneath the covers of an unfamiliar bed, in an unfamiliar room. It is light outside the window. I have overslept. It is morning. I prop myself on my left elbow and check my watch. It is barely nine -- p.m. -- "2059" on my digital dial. The light is from the risen moon. I fall back onto the pillow. Without my glasses the room is in soft focus. Someone is standing beside the bed. My mind returns, for now. "Aaley?"

"Sh," she says and gets into bed with me. She is naked, too.

She slides her body on top of mine, presses her pubis against mine. "I come with you," she says. I'm not sure of the syntax. She brushes her breasts across my chest, then touches her lips lightly to mine. "I am your connection," she whispers. So far I can feature this connection thing. So far, it seems very positive.

She presses her lips firmly against mine. They taste faintly of lipstick, a cheap taste that sends a shiver of cheap lust through me. Her black-flecked eyes are riveted to mine. She brushes her nose across mine. A sliver of ice is driving its way up my insides. There is a distant tingling in my scrotum. Can it be death? Is my time come? "I come with you," she says, again. I don't understand the syntax. But the death thing has me terrified. I am getting hard.

She is kissing me, pressing hard against my lips, as if trying to close off all outside air, all oxygen that doesn't pass first through her. She is rubbing her cunt on my cock. My mind is an insane jumble. What the fuck is going on here? This is out of my control. *I* am not in control. Yeah, right, like when was I ever *in* control?

Aaley works the underside of her tongue down the bridge of my nose. Her lips suction over my chin. She nips at my neck, then walks her lips down my chest to my cock. She slides her mouth over it and begins an erotic suc-

18

tion. She is not just riding her lips along the shaft like my other, unskilled lovers; she is using a kind of light suction that is drawing the sap from deep inside me, up into the plumbing. Ready the main torpedoes.

She rises up on her knees, does a one-eighty, drops her knees on either side of my head and resumes sucking on my cock. Her long, straight, black, black hair brushes my inner thighs. She swings the strands across my feet, like a lifeguard throwing a rope to a dying swimmer. The feathery touch is incredibly sensual. Her hair wipes the moisture from my feet.

There is no awkwardness; a flower child at work. Where did she learn this shit? Where did she come from? I am twice her age and more. The young ones will have young men. They will not understand. Not this young one. Come on, really, how old is she? She is old, buddy, . . . old. Then, I will show her how to die. No -- she will show me. Her mother will show up. Her father will show up and kill me. Her father is dead.

Her cunt is inches above my mouth. So far I have just been the victim, but the strong, erotic smell of her sex is too much for me. The smell is delicious, stronger around the cunt of this young girl, the lingering residue of urine, the mist of oxides of nitrogen. Nitrogen and oxygen, the principal components of the air I breathe. I cannot live without them. I raise my head and lick the petals of her cunt. The heavy smell transforms to the thick sweet taste of her vaginal milk. She moans, but continues to suck. I can feel the sap rising in me. Much too quickly. I can't do this. I can't continue. I can't stop. A quiver shoots through me. She senses it and dismounts, leaving my cock a wet, gleaming tower in the moonlight. She drops on her back and beckons to me to come on top of her. She looks beautiful in the lunar light. Her hair a covering of crochet

19

across the pillow. All of this is out of my hands. I wash my hands of this. I mount her.

      Her legs are all the way back, she is holding them behind her knees. Her cunt is straight up, my cock coming straight down. I am stroking inside her. She is slick as wet glass. Her face is childlike, a finger is in her mouth. I am dizzy. Again, I am getting close. Again, she senses it. She pushes me off. I plop down onto the mattress, into the bed. She rolls over and up onto her hands and knees, tosses her hair onto her back, it falls over her shoulders, exposing the liquid smooth surface of her skin: white silver in the moonlight. She parts her knees. I roll, then rise to my knees. Her cunt atop the triangle of her legs is soft wool, creased up the middle. I part the black hairs, expose the blood-red meat. I slide in. I am fucking her from behind. With each withdrawal stroke, the brown inner lip of her cunt clings to the shaft of my cock like a suction cup. It is the same feeling she'd created with her mouth. How does she do that? Her cunt paints the shaft of my cock with mucous. Her ass is polished steel. It gleams in the moonlight. She reaches under and begins fingering her clitoris. The soft brushes of her fingers feather my testicles, send incredible shiver-pulses through my scrotum. I watch her cunt sliding along my cock. I watch her asshole tighten and loosen. I feel the release coming. I expect her to change positions, but this time she will let me have my pleasure. Her cunt lips smack with each stroke. The sound is driving me crazy. My cock is painted with her juices. I am looking across the incredibly smooth expanse of her back. White silver in the light. Her crotch is a soft pad of steel wool patting against my thighs.

      "Come," she whispers, "Come inside me, come become me."

I thrust into her cunt. Hold it there. I shoot into her in an incredible, explosive release. Her asshole puckers, tightens, releases. She yelps. She is coming. She pushes her buttocks back until they press against my abdomen. She holds her ass tight against my belly until my cock is spent, then she grinds out the rest of her orgasm. I feel the final quivers of her vaginal wall. She smells heavy of woman. She reaches under and strokes my testicles with the tips of her fingers. It tickles.

"Success?" she asks.

"Yes," I answer. "Yes."

"Of course."

She pulls off. Pushes me down onto the pillow. Squats over me. Holds her cunt lips open. I am looking straight up into the blood-rich, red-brown petals in the soft forest of her pubic hair. I love the lack of symmetry, the irregularity, the complexity of form. Her cunt is a metaphysical statement, a chaotic design, comprehensible only to a superior designer. A thread of milky cum slides down to her lips. She holds the position. A viscous droplet in milky white with a touch of yellow from her pee, resting on the soft ridge of her cunt lips, it collects and adds weight, falls. I catch it on my tongue, liquid silver in the moonlight. It has her taste now added to mine, the powerful taste of her sex. I lick her cunt clean. The taste is a narcotic. I spiral out among the spheres.

I dress in silence. Words are useless now. She lays there, watches me, communicates somehow. Not bad for an old fuck, I want to say.

You ain't dead yet, she answers.

Yet.

She lets me out without a word. There are no words that work. Words or works, the great debate. Too late for that shit. Anyway. I hear the latch click into place,

21

but she doesn't engage the bolt. Does she not fear death? I can only guess.

04

I am in Cap d'Antibes on leave from my job as a
munitions officer assigned to a fighter squadron at the Avi-
ano Air Force Base in Italy. I am sitting at a table at the
outdoor restaurant behind the Motel Baie des Anges where
I've been staying. I am sipping a beer and scribbling in my
journal. It is the early Vietnam years. I have been extremely lucky, being assigned to the Italian Alps. It probably has something to do with a psychological test I was
given just after getting my commission. One question
asked about long term objectives. I'd answered, "poet."
The Air Force didn't want poets launching aircraft in Viet
Nam -- at least not those who wanted to be poets *before*
they'd become drug-addicted. I'd joined the Air Force to
skirt the Army draft. I didn't want my balls blown off slog-
ging through the jungles of the Mekong River. Despite Italy's safe distance from the war zone, we have been treated
to continuous "combat-readiness" drills: preparing for a
ground attack in the jungle. We launch the aircraft at all
cost, then worry about our own survival, on the bare apron
of concrete, devoid of cover from even the fighter aircraft
we have just launched, beneath wings filled with kerosene.
The only place left to take cover is the tiny circle of my
own shadow. I have spent weeks perfecting the art of hiding in the small circle of my own shadow.
   She is walking on the beach, a black dot oscillating
in the liquid air, against the shimmering alabaster of a huge
building unfurled like a frozen sheet at the point of land
which defines the far end of the beach. She is stepping
through a vacuum, with the delicacy of a hummingbird,
threading the spaces between atoms, displacing nothing.

23

She is wearing a black business suit and white blouse and strolling between the lounge chairs of bare-breasted women like a missionary assigned to Sodom or Gomorrah. She is the most beautiful woman I have ever seen.

I have a persistent headache from the beer, the sun and too many cigarettes. I am taking the last drag on a Marlboro and she is standing before me.

"You are burning holes in your lungs," she says. She says it because she is death's enemy and I am committing suicide.

"I only breathe when I have to," I respond. I feel the need to quip. I get an immediate sense that I am out-gunned intellectually.

"We have to talk," she says. She takes my hand, gently nurtures me out of the chair and leads me inside.

Inside.

"Please refrain from smoking when we are together," she says as I finger the pack in my breast pocket. Her voice is authority.

"I didn't realize we were . . . together." I release my finger grip. The pack slips to the bottom of my pocket.

"You do lack a certain level of awareness," she persists.

"I've never denied that."

I want to fuck you. I mean I really want to fuck you.

"I'm sure."

She does not equivocate. I like that. When you break them, they fall like a shattering stone. The gain is short term. The pleasure goes out of the game. I need to formulate a strategy but I don't want her to break, not this one.

"You need to get in touch."

Yes, touch.

"Say something. I will not read your thoughts."

24

"That's wise. I think."

"How long are you here?"

My opening to force the issue. "Tonight," I lie.

"I guess I'll have to accommodate that."

We agree to meet for dinner. She says she'll buy if I don't smoke. I make no promises, detailed plans. I need to respect the flow, this time. But if it carries her downstream, I will die. She moves right from dinner to my small, hot room with the Murphy bed, and the shutters that open onto the beach, and the small plastic table lamp, and I fear that it has gone south on me, but instead, it is the definitive night of my early adulthood.

It is an animal encounter. A realism. It is codified in the exchange of bodily fluids, internally and externally, a globuled dance of micro-organisms. Eminently real. Words cancel here; few are attempted. None exchanged. We have vectored together, the join-point of two non-parallel routings. The null point of the real. The gateway to the reverse V.

The next morning, we walk the beach, a few words passing between us. A union has been struck, we both know it. It is based upon need, we both understand that as well. I need someone who will put up with my bullshit. She needs someone who requires an infusion of life, on a regular basis. But it will never work as well as it did last night. It will grow ever-more-difficult. We both know that.

A vendor has spread his blanket on the sand in front of us and, before we can pass, dangles a charm bracelet before my eyes. He is a black man, at least black is the color of his skin. His features are thin, not congruent to his skin, stereotypically speaking. He is a white man painted black.

"C'est un poisson d'or," he says.

25

A tiny fish charm dangles from a chain of cheap gold.

"How much?" I ask.

"Hundred francs," he says. His eyes are yellow, cat's eyes, or the eyes of a victim of liver disease.

I shake my head and turn to go.

"How much you geeve me?"

"Fifty?"

"Oh, monsieur. Eets gold."

"Fifty."

He hands it to me.

I pay the fifty francs. The cat man folds the note I've given him and slides it into the pocket of his shirt. He hisses something I do not understand and I kneel and place the chain around Oomieka's ankle. He wants the woman I am with. He is convinced he can elevate the passion-exchange to heights she could never achieve with me. (He has no idea what he is up against.) If there is an issuance, the genealogical possibilities are . . . frightening. His eyes dismiss me as we proceed along the sand.

She returns to medical school in England; I return to preparations for war. She wears the ankle bracelet, when we are married three months later. She is pregnant with our child. We dispose of it in a clinically acceptable fashion. She becomes a doctor; I never fire a shot in anger. We see each other over long weekends or during her academic breaks, when I take leave. I have no idea who my wife is, only that the sight of her fills me with desire. Her desire for me seems more . . . calibrated, with the occasional burst of intensity, like the bounce of the mercury column on a blood-pressure gauge. Between visits, I fuck around with the locals.

The bracelet, she has long since retired to her jewelry box for safe-keeping.

26

"I've been thinking, Max," Oomieka says, "the kids and I . . . we need a breather."

"You're going home to mom?"

"For a couple of weeks. You wear me out when you're like this --"

"Like what?" I interrupt. "I'm me. The way I always am."

"No, Max. You're the poet again. The killer poet. The one for whom no words suffice. The one who finds destruction the only solution, the biggest attraction. In your mind, you are over-turning all the bookshelves in all the libraries of the world, because everything ever written is shit. You are tearing through every page, running through every line to find the one that works. The only one. The thing is . . . there is no number for you. I used to think you'd reduced it all to one, but now I know the number is zero."

"Number? Zero?"

"Max, God, don't play dumb. We've had this talk before. You're looking, you said, for number one. Just that and nothing more."

Is she doing it now? Is it her or me? Am I rearranging her words in my insanity?

"Oomieka, you're my anchor. Without you, I'm hopelessly adrift."

"You're adrift whatever. You only circle me, Max. You just come in for gas, food and lodging."

"But I know you're there."

"Where, Max? Where?

" . . . There."

27

She needles a few stitches to a flower petal. "We're only gone a couple of weeks. Mom will enjoy the girls for the holidays."

"And I am here alone?"

"You hate the holidays."

It's true.

"And always find a way to ruin them for the girls."

Fuck 'em.

Fuck 'em?

I can't . . . can I?

"While we're away, you can return to the wild."

Yesss.

I fall silent, a few moments.

We are in the family room watching TV. We do that evenings, between nine and ten, when I've managed to make it home that early. The TV fare is typically ridiculous. I break my promise and begin to criticize the plotlines. The show ends. I unleash my full, mocking fury.

"Endings," Oomieka says in annoyance. "Why must you always rewrite the endings?"

"Because they are never right."

"And you know the right one."

I say nothing, of course. I don't want to upset her further.

"Why don't you just let it be, then?"

"I can't."

I go to my room to write . . .

In a room in a motel in Cap d'Antibes, we fucked
     in the middle of the night,
by the light of a plastic table lamp, on a Murphy
     bed,
near a window with the shutters open to let in
the steamed breeze.

28

It was dark outside along the sea and I could feel
the eyes of the fishermen on us,
like invisible hands groping along my back,
toward the warm, wet smell of Oomieka's sex.
I could hear the slap of their nets on the water,
slithering down around the finger fish
they trapped for bait further up the food chain.
Oomieka's hot, oily skin glistened in the lamplight,
her legs hiked back,
her heels spurring my arms,
the quiet curves of her thighs and torso,
the fulfilled promise of her cunt.
Short burps of her breath counterpointed the grunts
          of the fishing men,
the death rattle of the finger fish.
Am I invading, I wondered, a very private moment
          for the finger fish?
Why,
I wondered,
had I left the shutters open?
Was it that the hour was very late?
But I did not close the shutters
and I ran my hands over the wonderful flesh
that lined either side of Oomieka's cunt
and we went on fucking.

05

I am acknowledged by my colleagues only at the minimal level demanded by common courtesy. They don't like me and avoid contact with me, except when protocol dictates they must. The lone exception is Simeon Golan, chair of the English Department's Graduate Studies Program.

Golan is a Princeton-educated black man from Guyana, who left as part of the brain drain that fled years of corrupt and grossly incompetent Marxist regimes which grew as a reaction to centuries of British arrogance, followed by a misguided strategy of playing off the Soviet desire to gain pockets of influence in the West. He is a large, round-faced man with shiny skin that glistens behind a thin layer of moisture which gives him the appearance of being made of onyx. He has a fine mind and a baritone voice which he loves to employ to dramatic effect. He speaks as if every sentence were a line from Shakespeare, offered at the climactic moment in the drama.

Simeon is carefully complimentary of my poetry, but he does not do it to stroke me. He strokes no one. So all I can conclude is that he sees something in it. He is my audience of one, which is not all that great, because Simeon is, for the most part, a pain in the ass. In terms of my treatment vis a vis my colleagues, Simeon assumes an egalitarian stance. It is, however, less a function of any inherent bent toward fair play and more a result of his need to exercise his sense of superiority. He sees in the state of tension between me and my fellows the opportunity to demonstrate his control, in the name of even-handedness. He is a descendent of black slaves, with the power over white men. He likes to break balls. He uses me. I know it. He freely admits to it. Whatever his motivation, he is useful to me. I let him play his little games. I give him what he requires.

"You know I like you, Max," he is saying. "I don't want to see you flushing your career down the toilet."

He sucks his lips back into his mouth with a smacking sound, then sips the thin-piss coffee he brews every morning in a four-cupper he keeps on the credenza behind his desk. I know he likes it much stronger, but he is too cheap to brew it that way. He never offers his guests a cup. Once, when I had a splitting headache, I asked for one. He said he didn't have enough for another cup.

This line of questioning -- even when it is not posed as a series of questions, he is questioning -- this line of questioning is heading somewhere. I could be direct in my response, attempt to cut to the chase, but you don't do that with Simeon. He will get where he is going in his good time. "You don't *like* me, Simeon," I respond. "No one likes me. You know if they can me, you won't have anyone who actually listens to your self-laudatory harangues."

"I do the listening, Max. You do all the talking."

Not true, of course, but I humor him. "You've never protested."

He smiles. "Your painful analyses of life as we know it are too entertaining."

"You just want to hear about my sexual exploits, under the guise of an interest in my poetry. And even though you know I don't separate fantasy from fact, the poems excite you."

31

He smiles again. "Actually, Max, it's all part of the dossier. I could have you packed and out of here in an hour."

"But you won't because you know I don't give a shit and you're waiting for me to develop a dependency so you can manipulate me like you do the rest of the weaklings you have sucking up to you."

Again, the smile, but this time I detect a degree of strain. I have succeeded in nudging him a bit off center. "Don't stop being so entertaining," he says. "There's no other reason to justify your existence."

I throw him a palm's up. "*Eyeth. Eyeth.* I am who I am. I do what I can."

"Speaking of your sex life," he says, "tell me about the coed."

It is a curveball. Obviously the pitch he's been waiting to throw. "She is helping me with my poem," I lie. It is all I can manage on short notice.

"We have rules about coeds, but I know you know that."

"Rules? She's auditing my Milton class," I lie again. "I assume that's within the rules."

"I'm not talking about administrative procedures." I try a shift to academics. "She is quite bright."

The smile frays at the corners like snapped twine. "I don't see you needing input from a twenty-year-old."

He is slipping into his investigatory mode. The full-court press is on. I assume my role as defendant. I have no choice. Once again, I opt for diversion. "I like her name: Altagloria."

He stops amid-sip, pins me with his gaze. It's the look I get when he thinks I'm holding back. Or when he knows something I don't. He blows a ripple across the grey liquid and replaces the cup in the saucer. "Her name is Margaret Montgomery," he says. "She's been kicked out of seven different schools. She fucks her professors, first for grades, then for cash."

My brow furrows predictably, the reaction he's anticipated, the victory he requires. But it is brief. I regain my composure -- albeit with some difficulty -- for the obvious counter. "Why would you check into her background?"

"It's my job to know what's going on in my department. And she's in there . . . for now." He sips, then pauses dramatically. Suddenly I realize the blatant sensuality of the play of his lips with the surface of the hot liquid. This whole fucking thing is turning him on. "Eventually," he resumes, "they go out the door with her, seven of your colleagues in far-off English Departments, now floating freely in the upper layers of the academic ether."

I am undeterred in my resistance. Take the high road. "She cannot fuck me for grades because I am not grading her."

He knows that's so. What he wants to know is if I'm getting any, anyway. He'll have to wait . . . for the poem.

"She is quite bright," I repeat, to render any peripheral bullshit irrelevant, and to piss him off, of course. "She connects with my message, has tapped into my veins."

"You're fucking with your future," he counters limply.

"I have no future."

I rise and head for my office.

33

06

Gravity has been pulling at her breasts. They have begun to look like those sacks of sand appended to the sides of hot-air balloons. I've nicknamed her Bags. Not to her face, of course.

She is on the phone.

At least she is calling the office, but I do not want a pattern of calls, even here. She just needs to talk, she says, nothing in particular on her mind. She just needs to let the words come out, see where they go.

"You do that to me, Max," she says. "I say different words when I'm with you. Words I didn't know I knew. My feelings come out, Max. My emotions become words."

She is almost giddy, looking for reinforcement that I am pleased she is pleased with this inspiration she says I provide her. I am not. She senses it. Crashes. Ruth does that.

"I'm happy you can have that kind of release, Ruth." It is just something to say. She is not in my thoughts.

"Walter is acting strangely," she says. It gains my full attention, involuntarily.

"How so?"

"I think he suspects something. He wanted to bed me this morning."

"He *is* a man, Ruth."

I imagine her in the morning, in her woolly bath-robe with the circles of grease from countless egg-fries, her greyed-pink slippers, her morning breath intensified by a two-pack-a-day habit, and Walter cooing, "I got the hots for ya, Bags."

Walter is an annoyance. He is in the way. He takes up space. Once an electrician, he is on disability for a fall through the unfinished floor of an office tower he was working on. He was on his way to a break. At first, they thought he had broken his back, but there was nary a cracked nor herniated vertebrae. Nonetheless an evaluation board determined he'd wrecked his back, so he was awarded full disability. He makes more than I do to hang out in the local sports bar from dawn to midnight, except on Wednesdays when he attends union meetings. He holds some kind of title with the local local for which he collects an additional stipend and for which he also does nothing. He doesn't even show up most of the time, because on Wednesdays, under the guise of attending his union meeting, he attends his "union" meeting, freeing Ruth for her union meeting with me. Walter is a big zero. He does nothing but take up space. He doesn't even service his wife. I do that. For which I get nothing.

Whenever I think about Walter I reckon him dead. He serves no purpose and he is in the way, an annoyance to me, albeit minor. He is, however, a potential problem of major proportions should I get careless or should Ruth decide to utilize him to threaten me.

Walter is overweight and mostly inactive, except when he has to do things like lift the room airconditioner into and out of the window, which he does with terrible technique, lifting with his back instead of his legs. And he has high blood pressure, so I'm hoping for a killer heart attack or a debilitating stroke. Ruth likes him the way he is. He spends so little time with her and he pays the bills. That works for Ruth, but fuck Ruth. Next Wednesday.

35

Maybe I'll be motivated by then. And maybe Walter will be dead.

"He never wants it in the morning."

"Meaning?"

"He wanted to see if it had been used."

"He can tell?"

"I *was* a bit sore, but I didn't show it. I just gritted my teeth."

She is giving him too much credit.

"That was wise," I answer.

"And painful."

Ruth is delivering her message: nothing is without consequences.

"His blood pressure was through the roof. I mean his face was red as a beet."

"Then, I guess we'd better quit for a while," I respond.

"Not really," she says, "but we do need to be careful."

"I thought we were being careful."

"Of course. But extra careful."

Fuck Walter. What could he do? Beat the shit out of Bags? Come after me?

It's your out, asshole. Get out.

"What's the matter?"

"You felt the need to tell me this, Ruth."

"I told you the words come out."

"The words are telling us something, now aren't they?"

"They're telling us to be careful." The sentence is ragged. She has said too much. I have said too little. She is losing control. I am losing my grip.

"Let's talk in a few days, a week would be better."

"A week?"

It would wipe out a Wednesday.

"I think it's best."

"Oh, Max. You're such a worry wart. It's nothing, just words."

"Words have meaning, Ruth." I am playing professor with her. She hates it when I get pedantic. To her, I'm just a cock.

"I know," she stumbles. "I --"

"Look, I've got to get to class."

"I --"

"Ruth, I've got to go."

"All right," she snaps. "Go."

She hangs up.

I mean I do have my fucking class, don't I?

07

She is there, focusing her beam.

It is my graduate class in Milton. Late-comers drift in.

I am beneath the sea, above a reef. A long, thin light ray is burning a circle in a formation of brain coral. Now the entire sphere is blood red, robin's breast orange, saffron, white fire. It explodes, scattering brain fragments across the beam. Particles of dust, dancing in the light. Thoughts. Words. Congestive. Eurodollars. Crack. Crawl. Pee, procreate. Lungs. Air. Air. A fetus floats in womb water. Warm womb water. There is the smack of flesh against flesh. An infant cries.

"Professor?"

The clock on the wall has no hands.

"Professor?"

The hands appear. Circles in the center of each palm, about the size of a penny, the color of the leaves of the copper beech in my backyard.

It is ten after the hour.

"Are you all right?"

She is gone.

"The Areopagitica. It is not what it says. (Shit!) Of course it is what it says. It says it, doesn't it? Words say things, don't they? Mean things, don't they?"

"Professor, are you OK?"

She was there, wasn't she?

A stream of words is falling over my lips.

"The Areopagitica. OK. So who has read and understands the assignment?"

No hands.

Look, ma, no hands. The clock has no hands.
"OK. Let's get more basic. Who has *read* the assignment?"

No hands.

I am suddenly aware of the antagonistic tone in my voice dying in the dead air of the stagnant room. This room is nowhere, going nowhere. But I am in the power position. I am enjoying it. Today, I will make them suffer.

"Then who has *not* read the assignment."

Still no hands.

"OK, good. Let's see if we can use these obvious contradictions. Try to follow me. What is Milton telling us? Books are useful, yes?"

A few tentative nods.

I stare down the nodders.

". . . But then he tells us books are useless, no?"

Utter confusion.

"Man achieves virtue via books, but books, in and of themselves, do not contain virtue, so how does man achieve virtue? Or perhaps he cannot. Who will explain?"

No takers.

"OK, I will. Try to follow. The Areopagitica is Milton's tract on pre-publication licensing, or, in a broader sense, his argument against prior censorship, or, to put it positively, in favor of freedom of expression, or, in terms of the U.S. Constitution, freedom of the press. In the Areopagitica, he argues that while books may not be virtuous in and of themselves, they assure man's movement toward virtue."

I pause for effect, survey the room, raise my eyebrows, use body language to try to elicit a response.

"Well? Comments? No?"

No movement.

39

"Yehs?" I drag out the word, get a handful of head-nods. (A headful of hand-nods?)

"No!" I snap. "How could a book that in and of itself lacks virtue move a man toward virtue? A book that is, let's say, untrue, like the Apocryphal Gospels, would lead a man away from virtue. Yehhhs?"

No reaction. Total intimidation.

"No! The Apocryphal Gospels were apocryphal only in terms of their relationship to the accepted, orthodox texts, not necessarily their messages. So, we have no way of determining whether a book will lead you toward or away from virtue. Yehhs? No! Well, maybe yes; maybe no. Perhaps the book is not the determinant. Perhaps it is the man. But if it is the man and not the book, or by extension, it is the man and not the experience, then is Milton saying men are born virtuous? Or unvirtuous? Or some are and some aren't?"

Utter, total confusion. Stirrings, faces riveted upon desks, or, lower still, shoes and shoelaces. Dumb fucks. Somebody say something. Someone. I want to grind you to a bloody, bone-gritty pulp.

"Maybe . . . " I soften my tone and survey the room. "Maybe it's Milton who is full of shit. Maybe he is fucking with our heads. Maybe he is demonstrating how fucking smart he is and what dumb fucks all the rest of us are."

The amplitude of my voice has risen beyond the bounds of proper classroom decorum.

"Where is the truth here? Is it in books? Is it in men? Is it anywhere? Is it nowhere? Is it --"

"Perhaps it is in the quest."

She is back.

"Perhaps it is not a static element to be dug out of books. Perhaps it is there inside the . . . woman, or at least the potential for it is, and the quest nurtures it."

"W-well," I stutter, "if it is not in the man and it is not in the book, then what about this one? What about the Areopagitica? Is Milton telling us his own book is a lie?"

She smiles. "You said it. I didn't."

"Well, then, going with your read, I'd have to say the Areopagitica is a lie only if we look at it as a static entity . . . as a book. If we view it as an element in movement, as something that moves toward the truth, then it is not a lie."

"But," she counters, "if it is not a lie, then must it be the truth? Or, can it be some part one and some proportion the other?"

"B-but . . . "

She has taken over the class. She has wrested the power from me: the point *I* was going to make, as Milton was using his essay to demonstrate that no single component could embody the truth, I was using the class --

She is gone.

I am decomposing. Leaves falling into the river. Water the color of Coca-Cola. The room is a dark universe of dinner plates, floating free in space. Round eyes, disembodied. There is a buzz in the room. An electric hum. I refocus for a fraction.

They get it.

They fucking get it. For an instant. Then it is gone. The bell rings and they are gone.

I sit. Await their return.

They aren't coming back.

41

08

One of the reasons I continue to smoke is because my colleagues disapprove. There is a designated smoking area in the faculty lounge, actually a designated table with a single chair -- for me. While they know the university has designated smoking areas to separate those who do not from secondary smoke, the theory doesn't work in practice because, of course, my noxious, toxic gases float about the entire lounge in wisps and eddies. I am killing them softly with my exhaust fumes. Predictably, my colleagues fill first the seats at tables furthest from me. Then, they engage in conversation of carefully modulated amplitude, sending across the smoke-filled gorge that separates us just those fragments of language meant to engage me, on their terms. I, of course, ignore most of these intrusions, responding only when my fellows become convinced ignorance is my strategy. Mostly, I respond when no response is expected, to those conversational exchanges not meant to be shared with me. I have an uncanny sense for determining what they are talking about, supplemented by intelligence via my frequent exchanges with Simeon Golan.

Now, for example, Andy Dagliesh and Bart Carp are deep in dialectic about the role of the teacher, the subject of an upcoming conference at the university; it's to be an examination of the teacher as power figure. I am a total non-entity during this round. I'd been the object of a merely perfunctory salutation when they arrived, then the punch/counter-punch began. I am puffing smoke in great clouds, a blatant play for attention. I am especially shameless on one of my weak days.

Of the two, Dagliesh dislikes me the less. He is a man who tries to be pleasant most of the time. It is a posture created to defend his weak character. He is a tall, slight, breakable man, draped in yellow skin and a stack of dense dishwater hair. He is the lone colleague who will engage me in conversation from time to time, but only when we are isolated one-on-one. He does it to neutralize a thickening of the tension were we to sit silently. His particular area of expertise is modernist poets. He did his dissertation on T.S. Eliot. When we talk, we talk of my poetry. He provides, after all, expert criticism. I am sure the intelligence he gathers thus provides the grist for critiques of me when he rejoins his comrades. He cuts loose of me as soon as anyone else enters the room.

Bartolomeo Carpozzi is a simple read. He is an asshole. His nom-de-plume is Bart Carp, a label he felt was necessary when he began writing narrow-focus, narrow-audience novels attempting excruciatingly probing portraits of singularly uninteresting characters, whose progenitors in all the elements of their failed successes had already been probed ad nauseam by better-selling authors. Carp saw his much-narrower audience as far more cognizant of superior work. He would remain loyal to them until some whiff of popular success promised to expand the percentage of adoring females beyond the two or three nubile former students he was already boffing. Academic articles, of course, were bylined Bartolomeo Carpozzi, Ph.D. He was no more skilled at writing scholarly pieces and they were harder to place, which was excruciatingly painful for Carpozzi, since he was basically a lazy son-of-a-bitch with a mediocre writing talent.

It is at Bart Carp that I direct my comment. I'd debated going for Andy, but I wasn't up to the skewed plea for guidance he'd direct at Bart. I wanted the horse's mouth. Ass?

"Nihil."

The word has the predictably disruptive effect. They are not sure where to go with the silence. They're not even sure what they've encountered. I am back to my smoke signals. It has become questionable whether I have even said anything. (I have, in fact, said nothing.)

Bart clitches.

"Nihil."

This time, they were almost ready. This time, it is clear that I have spoken.

"Did you say something, Max?" Bart asks. "Do you have something to contribute?"

"Nothing," I answer, smiling, puffing, dinching. "I have nothing to contribute." I end with the clipped "t". Silence is born, thickens.

That which is not cannot in anyway be something.[1]

I light up again, recede into my self-induced eruption. The buzz is restrung with occasionally decipherable singlets, doublets, quartets, triplets. I have lost interest, swirl a nimbus about my head, fly off like a bird honking among the billows. Light striped in shadow, the door opens, latches closed, leaving within the formidable form of Angelica Magnus, the colleague I most fear. She . . . is relentless. She favors neither B.C./A.D. nor me, but triangulates the distance between. Discussion is halted because Angelica, unlike me, does not play. She prefers the full-frontal approach, no bullshit, plunge the knife through the breastbone -- never, ever into the back. I admire her, actually.

Angelica is deeply involved in the subject of the upcoming conference. The relationship between teacher and student is a subject she takes very seriously. It is a dy-

44

namic she has been studying for years because, among all of us, she is teacher, in terms of both command of her subject matter and how that information is delivered to her students, or, as she might put it, how she helps students get in touch with what they already know. She has questioned the historically entrenched positioning of the teacher/philosopher, philosopher/king as the post of ultimate power and the student as that of ultimate vulnerability. I had once commented to her, without much aforethought, that the teacher-student relationship was the stripped down metaphor for life. She burst out laughing. "Life," she'd countered, "is the metaphor." You don't make comments to Angelica without aforethought.

Anyway, I put out my cigarette, pick up my copy of De Magistro, shuffle through it. I raise my eyes slightly to see what Angelica is doing. She is scribbling something on the top sheet of a pile of papers. I find the appropriate passage. "For who is so stupidly curious as to send his son to school in order that he may learn what the teacher thinks?"[2]

Only Angelica understands our role as catalyst. I want to convey that I understand she understands but alas, I don't have that kind of relationship with any of my colleagues.

She is flipping pages and pouring over the text. When she is so engrossed, I study her, alert to any shift in her attention which will expose what I am doing. Her smallish hands address the pile of papers as if it were precious parchment; the right anchoring the upper right corner, the ball of the index finger planing along the side to assure a smooth edge; the left directing a gold encased fountain pen that exposes neat rows of computer lettering for the careless thinking they represent. She betrays none of her thinking, this Angelica Magnus, no miniscule move-

45

ment of her lips pantomiming a word fragment, no lift of an eyebrow in response to a point well made. I am transfixed, riveted too long. Her eyes dart in my direction; mine run for cover.

And since after the speaker has reminded them, the pupils quickly learn within, they think they have been taught outwardly by him who prompts them. [3]

Let'ss discusss.

The planing finger increases the stroke frequency. Stops. Taps lightly the corner of the page pile, resumes its feathered strokes. She is aware of my intrusion. I seek, however, a truce. I need to talk, negotiate. I'm at a loss, cannot determine how I might proceed. Her composure is altered, trivially, but true, the wrinkle above her right eyebrow not positioned in response to words printed on the page. She knows not what to make of this. I am interrupting, but I sense it's something she finds useful.

During my pubescence, I used to walk, on rainy, misty afternoons, to the river, to listen to the round-faced demented girl howl her desire. I don't remember if I fucked her.

She is fixed on me.

The jury will disregard that last comment.

Both eyebrows V toward the bridge of her nose. It is a design to which I can relate. She returns to her papers momentarily. Reestablishes contact.

"So, Max," she says, "what's your take on all this?"

I cannot remember the last time she initiated contact.

I am stunned. Unable, immediately, to react. But I must ward off awkwardness.

I gather up books and papers and rise from my chair. "May I?"

She says nothing, delivers no gesture of welcome.

46

I walk the nine paces to her position. There is an empty chair opposite, no bare place on the table to put my things. I hesitate a moment to offer her an opportunity to clear some space. She does not. I drop my things on to the floor with a thud, take the chair, my back to Bert and Ernie[4].

"My interest," I begin, "if you are interested --" Her eyes soften. They are warm-brown. This time, they clearly invite. Again, I am caught off guard. "-- is in the larger issue."

A shiver fractures the thickness of the room. The conversation between my male colleagues is relegated to a sidebar. I am credentialed, for the present.

"You are a terrible teacher, Max," she says, "since you have made this personal."

"Based on . . . ?"

She smiles accepts my segue into the classical method.

"Observation, albeit fractional; feedback, from a variety of sources, albeit some questionable; gut instinct, usually very reliable."

She has abandoned the model. The desertion of methodology will inform my argument, but, "weak," is all I muster.

"Convince me," she counters.

So long as I have the floor, *I* am weak. "Guilty until proven innocent?" I opt momentarily to shift back to the dialectic. No response. "How . . . undemocratic. How unintellectual." I am at sea.

She smiles, again, but it lacks sincerity. Suddenly this whole thing is a bother. There is little or no history here, little potential in the wordplay. I panic. "Why do I bother?"

Her eyes brighten, briefly. "Yes."

47

Now a softness unfamiliar in this setting. Does she really want to know?

I soften.

"Fear," I respond, "of the unknown. It's what creates bullies."

"Your unfair advantage is your refuge."

"Refuge . . . interesting."

I can't help but assume the professorial pondering pose I truly despise. "It's a survival thing, now, isn't it?" I offer.

"How so?"

"My maintenance of a position of dominance is essential to interdicting your attack."

"You're right . . . " she answers. I sense we are not on the same page. ". . . It's a matter of weakness, not strength. Someone in a position of real power would not fear an attack."

"Are you saying my fear extends to my relationship vis a vis my students?"

"Their potential. Their unrealized energy."

"And therefore I seek to beat them into submission."

"Perhaps some ceremonial circumcision."

Stopped cold. "A la Yahweh?"

"You might say."

AB?

Naaaah.

"You need your students to complete the equation," she continues. "In effect, you are powerless without them. They are the source of your power, for without them, with whom would you contest, and do so with the virtual certainty that you will be victorious? To me, power in a condition of stasis is cowardice. It is only the assumption of power that requires courage. That is why once power becomes entrenched, it corrupts. No one can sustain the cour-

48

age required to maintain power in its truest sense, which would require continuous exposure to uncertain elements . . . at least no one in this world. You have to pull your pants down, Max, and expose yourself."

I want to challenge her, but I know that *is* what she does. She enters her class as the de facto power figure, but immediately throws herself into the fray.

"The excitement," she says, "is *not* knowing where it will end up."

No power. No control. Anti-knowledge. Pure excitement.

"Tell me, Angelica . . . "

"Yes."

"Why bother?"

She stops fucking with the papers, devotes full attention, again, only for an ill-defined moment. I raise my eyebrows vaudevilially and "hmmmm" to bid a response. She does not like this turn, hates it actually. I am drawing some neurotic pleasure from it, the turn, although I know not why. I'd thought I'd wanted her to . . . relate to me, somehow, but now all is lost and that . . . defines the odd pleasure.

"I have papers to grade," she says.

"Class dismissed?"

She dislikes my sarcasm, intensely. I understand, I have been asked to leave, but it is a demonstrative defeat I choose not to suffer. I think about lighting up a cigarette, but I am outside the authorized zone. That *would* provide the easy out. I choose not to take it. Stay. I return to my Augustine and allow the silence to be overtaken by the buzzing of Bart and Andy.

49

09

Oomieka and the kids are gone.

I don't remember saying good-bye. But it has become that way with us. The protocol is meaningless. I am alone for the holidays.

10

Esteban Dedalo Oriente is a friend of mine. His mother was an Irish actress; his father a Colombian painter. His name, like some of his better work, is a collage -- sometimes a collection of styles, other times of media, sometimes of both. He is an uncompromising artist, so he makes a living framing what his customers decide is art. Seldom do they decide on one of his paintings, collages or sculptures.

His shop, The Framing Objects Gallery, is at the far end of Main Street, near the boatyard and the auto body shop. It is not a good location for walk-in business.

I share some of my poetry with Esteban, but his appreciation for it is merely as a creative colleague.

"My mother would enjoy your poetry," is his recurring acknowledgment. His kiss-off.

Much of his work begins as an interpretation -- if understood as such only by him -- of the writings of Pablo Neruda, Federico García Lorca, Gabriel García Márquez, or one of the other twentieth-century writers in Spanish, living or dead. He begins greatly moved by the prose or poetry of one of these writers, then vaults off in the brush-stroke reaction to whatever image is roaring through his mind at any given point in time. His lone English-titled work of any magnitude is a large, three-canvas mural, he has been working on for more than two years, which he calls, "Work in Progress."[1] Whenever I comment on it, he says that James Joyce is the only creative writer of the twentieth century working in English. I tell him he is biased. He says art is bias.

In his painting, and particularly in his collages, Esteban is continually recreating reality. I tell him artists cannot resist playing God. He ignores the comment. Esteban sees God as speaking through him. Something external, a Neruda poem, one of Márquez's run-on sentences, triggers the epiphany and he is off. He just lets his muscles run. He says that is how I should write.

"You search too hard, Max," he is saying (he pronounces my name, "Mahx" or "Mox"). "You're wound too tight. Let it flow, man."

"You sound like an asshole when you speak in the American idiom." I get annoyed when anyone tells me how to work.

"That's a comebacker, Max. It doesn't address the issue."

"Comeback! Comeback! A comebacker is a one-hopper to the pitcher."

"That's what I meant."

"No it wasn't."

"You're embellishing now. It's frosting. You need to leave the cake out in the rain."

"You need to stop smoking whatever the fuck you're smoking."

"Have one, Max. It'll relax you."

He proffers a Marlboro Light. Hot air, no flavor. If you're gonna fuckin' smoke, smoke.

I take the cigarette. He takes one, lights two.

"You're wandering among the complexities," he resumes. "It's only adding to the confusion."

"I'm taking my cue from you."

"The complexity in my work flows from the simplicity of the elements. The simple elements converge to form the grand design. But I don't fight for it, like you do.

I let it come. It flows from the center of who I am, expanding outward."

"Like the universe flows outward from . . . ?"

"Perhaps."

"You are an insufferable egotist, Esteban."

He smiles, shakes his head, does not deny what I've said.

I want him to interpret one of my poems, but that seems unlikely given the ethereal territory he has staked out as his and his alone, and besides, I'll never ask him.

Besides me, he has two regular visitors: Ellen Barry and Ronald Richmann. Ellen Barry is a real estate broker who fancies herself the principal interpreter of Esteban's work; the only one who has managed to enter and wander about his disheveled mind. "It's all erotica," she says. "Rummaging about the attic of Esteban's mind is like leafing through piles of old skin books. Everything he paints is a variation of a vagina or a penis."

"She's dying to fuck me," Esteban says.

In my opinion, he's right. She has the hots for him, but he has a lovely wife, American, and two beautiful children. Theirs is the only relationship he has time for, given the amount of psychic energy he expends on his art, which has only intensified Ellen Barry's pursuit of him. It is shameful the way she sucks up to him, when he pays no attention to her blatant, pornographic comments. Lately, she has taken to telling him about her sexual encounters with other men, in graphic detail. They appear to have no effect on him. (They are having a powerful effect upon me.) I think one day she will die of the heat. I joke with Esteban that he is a closet homosexual, hiding behind a wife and children.

"What would you do differently?" he asks with an edge to his voice.

53

"Oh, I'd fuck her."

The other frequent visitor, Ronald Richmann, is a periodontist. He is also a would-be painter. He interprets biblical scenes, using severe geometric shapes, placed border to border like a modernistic mosaic. Painting is therapy for him. His wife and daughter were killed in an auto accident, for which Ronald blames himself. He was backing his car out of the driveway of his home when a delivery truck, speeding, crushed the right side. His wife was killed instantly; his daughter survived, even looked for about a week as if she might pull through, then suffered a heart attack, did not respond to attempts to resuscitate her, had no pulse for too many minutes, then on the last try with the defibrillator her heart cranked, but she was pronounced brain-dead, and Ronald opted to not keep her alive artificially. In effect, he killed his daughter twice. He had suffered a fractured collarbone in the crash, but recovered in a matter of weeks. He lives alone in an expensive condo on the sound, makes gobs of money on his dental practice and paints the prophets as squares and rectangles, trapezoids and triangles. He yearns for Esteban to approve of his work, but Esteban does not and Ronald knows he never will, but he presses on.

When we converge at The Framing Objects Gallery, we bring with us our distinctive agendas. Purity belongs to Esteban alone. He truly doesn't give a shit what anybody thinks. Deep down I hate him for having achieved this level of consciousness, but I am sucked along in his wake. This day I read him a poem I've written. I call it "The FOG." At first he is suspicious of the title, perhaps even insulted, but I've gained a level of his interest I've been unable to achieve with my other work. When I am finished reading the poem, he tells me he likes it. I can see it has played to his ego. A momentary lapse. When

54

the rest of the rhythm section arrives, he asks me to play it
one more time. We are gathered around the large work table he has built to work on his frames. I demur. He goads.
I demur again. Ronald asks (nicely). I shake my head. Ellen whines. I decline. There is a degree of enjoyment in
this. Finally, I agree.

> Near the north end of Main Street,
> far from the principal business district,
> is the Framing Objects Gallery --
>
> a white hole.
>
> The terrestrial antithesis of the
> celestial,
> this one emits light,
> explodes light, churning
> with the colors of its kinetic energy.
> Here, Esteban paints.
> He cuts, he pastes, he collages,
> then he puts frames about the works:
> gold frames, lacquered frames, natural wood,
> burnished metal
> . . . frames!
> Not to define limits,
> but to extend his art.
> "Canción menor"[2]
> "Canto General"[3]
> "La tarde soltó su verde cabellera lírica"[4]
>
> Today, the outline of a woman's face, untitled,
> her eyes thin black ellipses, more delicate than
> usual,
> a swath of beige cloth across her cheek,

55

not the usual potential energy of sexuality.
A more sublime moment for El Oriente.
The drying paints of yesterday
now swirl across a small, unprimed canvas,
blues and yellows leaking through.
"Tempestad":
a giant wave, a doomed sailboat, the captain escap-
                    ing into a square, lighted tunnel, through the canvas.
Here,
three small works titled, "Under Water's,"
an uncharacteristic attempt in English.
When I tell him the title is ungrammatical,
he asks that I correct the grammar.
I decline.

Truth need not obey the rules of grammar.
And light, certainly, is unrestrained.
The poem is a fraud, of course, a brochure. I want
Esteban to interpret one of my poems so I've poemed him
and his work. Corollarily, I feel he will take a greater inter-
est in my poetry if he has a vested interest in its celebration.
I celebrate myself, I sing myself,
And what I assume you shall assume . . .
I celebrate the victory
the holidays
the feast days
the mass
myself.[5]
"Well that was entertaining," Ellen Barry says.
"Yes, thank you," says Ronald Richmann.
I imagine Ronald interpreting one of my poems.
For an instant I see Aaley as a collection of geometric
shapes, but they are not flattened in two dimensions as
Ronald would have painted them. Instead they flutter like

56

wind chimes or a Calder mobile, in a half dozen plains of perspective. It is working actually, then it disappears.

Ellen Barry sees something revealing in "The FOG." Perhaps I've uncovered the side of Esteban she'd been seeking. Perhaps my poem has exposed this, the way poems sometimes do. It is the clue she's been searching. She assumes a position between Esteban and me. I get mostly her back. It is her most familiar posture re me. The cutting-horse stance. She engages Esteban, sottovoce. Ronald and I do not exist.

The front door opens and in walks a woman carrying a cardboard tube. I watch Esteban watch her the way he watches every customer who enters. She walks past two dozen of his most outrageous paintings without granting so much as a glance. She has an agenda, nothing else matters. At the counter which separates the four of us from her, she unfurls an oil painting she has purchased in the Caribbean. It is ersatz Haitian naïf. She launches into an explanation of Haitian painting canned for her by whoever sold her this weak representation. Esteban listens patiently, without engaging her. He is an expert on the subject, has used elements of the best of the school in his more ambitious work, examples of which hang invisible on the walls all about her. Esteban suggests mattings and frames. She rejects them all with condescending comments, finally deciding upon a combination of her own choosing, then argues about the price, which is two hundred twenty dollars. I am guessing it is twice what she paid for the painting, which is twice what she should have paid and ten times what the vendor paid the artist. For her benefit, and with exaggerated punctuation, Esteban measures the components again, recalculates the price, turns the calculator toward her so she can see the 2 2 0. She smirks.

57

"How much you geeve me?" Esteban says, in his best flea market voice.

"Well, I don't know," she answers, taken aback by his affectation. "It's just . . . it's just more . . ."

He gives her no quarter, staring her full in the face.

She scans the rest of us for a moment, realizing only then that she is seriously outnumbered, understanding only then that she is in unfriendly territory.

"More than you wanted to spend?" he resumes, more to move the transaction along than to allow her any breathing space. "How much did you want to spend? I'll show you some samples in that price range."

She is fidgeting with her handbag, then yields. "How much of a deposit do you require?"

"Oh . . . ten percent."

She pulls a twenty from her purse, holds it for a few moments.

"That's twenty-*two* dollars," he says.

She pulls out a five. He gives her her change.

"When will it be ready?"

"Oh . . . a week."

The smirk is permanently affixed. She wants to press him for an earlier day, but stops herself.

"Would you like it sooner?" he asks. "It's just that I don't like to rush *my* work."

"No," she says, "no, a week will do."

She turns and heads for the door. Just before she reaches it, she stops, approaches one of the paintings -- "Cuerpo de Mujer"[6] She studies it a moment, then steps back, is suddenly aware of it as a single element in a vast assembly. "Did you buy out the entire production of this artist?" she asks.

"Oh, jes," Esteban answers, "all of eet."

"Interesting," she says, bending at the waist and studying the lower border of one. "Interesting, but over-priced."

She leaves.

She is an awful woman, with a fuckable ass.

11

I'm a sucker for a power cunt. It's why Aaley has been in control here from the start. I could smell it, her pussy. I knew it could be optioned. I let her run her game. And she was good, real good.

Now, I'm back.

I have her pelt. She cannot get it back. I'm back in charge.

Oomieka? Aaley holds the Oomieka card?

Like Oomieka gives a shit about what some twenty-year- old coed might say. It wouldn't be the first time. It won't be the last. We have this understanding. I don't rub her face in it. "Keep them out of my zone."

Aaley could penetrate the zone?

Only if I weaken. Only if I need her. Only if I have to connect, again . . . surrender her pelt.

"You're a prostitute."

"I wanted to make a few bucks . . . and besides, I like the fucks."

"That's the job description."

"They're not supposed to like it."

"That's a side issue. The money's key."

"You got you a freebie."

"You were my connection, remember?"

"Yes . . . of course."

I cradle the cat with my fingers again. "So then, what does that make me?"

Her lips again assume the perpendicular pudenda.

I am anticipating an answer, but mostly it is hope, a childish sentiment. "So, what's it all about, Aaley?" is all that I can muster.

"Hey, you're the wisest of the wise. You tell me."

"Where do you come up with this shit?"

She stares at me in hot rivets of green, burst vessels gushing from her eyes into my brain, sparking synapses off like a pack of firecrackers popping along the pavement, slivers of shaved-point bamboo, scratching around in the congealed Jello behind the concrete skull wall -- to root out the scream. I contemplate the face, explore the mind, the soul. Out of whom went seven devils. My eyes roll back and now I am Jesus dragging my cross. *Elohi, Elohi, lama shebaqtani?* I am sullied, sorry, slime.

"It's only that you took the time."

"What?"

"Hel-lo." She snaps her fingers, as if to wake me.

I shake the cobwebs into a neat, silken pile on the floor of my brain. "So, now I'm to understand, that through you, I've had perhaps a dozen other men to screw."

". . . Give or take a few."

"This ain't funny."

"And you?"

"Me?"

"How many do you do?"

"Just you."

"Phew." She shakes her head. "And lying, too. Murder, theft, . . . and lies, too."

"But you were my connection."

"The reason for the near-perfection."

"Near?"

She smiles her smile. "Act Two."

I am coming back from a distance. A great dis-tance.

"I rejected you?" It is my voice, hanging in the pun-gent air of her bedroom.

61

Her eyes are filled with a sorrow so deep I cannot begin to gage its depths. We are naked, now, recent of a hot, sticky coupling. Rejection seems foreign to the situation. Then again, it took me some time to get a handle on the connection thing. Rejection. I cogitate about rejection. Cogito ergo sum. She is studying me for any mental movement. Her look seems to be leading me somewhere.

"Another life?" I venture.

She cops that far-away look women develop into an artform, starting when they are very young, that you-just-don't-get-it, you-can't-see-beyond-the-words look.

"You're not one of those disciples of re-incarnation?"

The steady, unflinching look.

I release a disgusted breath. "This is it, Aaley. This ends, the song is over."

"But the melody lingers on."

"My rejection of you in some former life, corrupted your morals in this one?"

"Who said anything about corruption?"

"Well, then what?"

She tells the story of her recent past. She'd joined a commune in the southwest, drawn for some reason to the desert, then fell in love with the leader. She wanted to be his wife, but he eschewed any kind of formal marriage ceremony. He'd arrange a wedding that was recognized by the cult -- which was easy because he made the rules as he went along. But she wanted a real marriage. He said he was forbidden to marry by divine proclamation. When he told her his decision was final, she left, took the name Margaret Montgomery, bounced around from school to school, slept with professors to earn food money, changed courses, could not settle into anything. "I'd become very objective-

62

oriented. If I needed something, I did what it took to get it."

"Forgive me, I'm dense. I don't get the connection, so to speak."

"I didn't know you were here."

I study her a moment. She does not betray any insincerity in this concocted story. I shake my head. Her eyes light a smile. Suddenly my lids are heavy. She runs her hands over my body, down my legs, massages my feet. Sleep is overtaking me.

She is not here. I lie on the bed, naked, spread eagle. Play with myself, waiting for whatever the fuck she does when she leaves me here, interminably, to stare at the cracks in the ceiling above the world, rerun the film across the editing monitor behind my eyelids. My cock gets very hard. My eyes grow lid-heavy. Is this the objective, to make me fall asleep? Was it only just a dream. My lids grow heavier, I cannot seem to raise them. I nod off, I'm sure of it. I dream about fucking Aaley. Her legs all the way back, her cunt straight up, my cock coming straight down. Just like last time. I've seen this dream before. It needs a different ending. What? This will take some innovation. I am stroking inside her. She is smooth as dry skin. Her face is childlike, a finger in her mouth. Did that already. I am fucking her from behind. With each withdrawal stroke, the brown inner lip of her cunt clings to the shaft of my cock like an O-ring seal. Her cunt paints the shaft of my cock with the milky mucous. That, too. She asks me to fuck her ass. OK. This is new. I can go with this for a while. I don't answer her. I smile. She begs me to fuck her ass. I withdraw from her cunt. She moans. The hole is the mouth of a largemouth bass. She constricts it. It closes. I dip my finger into her cunt until it is dripping wet. I lubricate her asshole, then push my cock in and

give her a good, firm butt-fuck. Her ass is polished glass.
It gleams in the moonlight. I cum in her ass. It is so warm
and accommodating in there. As I withdraw, my cock
smells faintly of shit. It is not unpleasant. I push into her
cunt. I cum in her cunt. I cum on her back. I fuck her tits
and cum on her face. She cums in my mouth. I ask her not
to tell my wife, my daughters. All this will be our little secret, I tell her. I don't believe she will keep it a secret. I determine to work on an explanation for Aaley's mother, for
my wife, my daughters. None is immediately forthcoming.
I table it for another dream. I awake gripping my rock-
hard cock. I wonder if I've been asleep through all this.

We are in the bathtub. I am on my back. Aaley is
squatting over me. Did that last time, too. I'm looking
straight up at her cunt. Waiting. Her form blocks the
bright white light of the heat lamp. I'm stroking my cock.
The anticipation is electric. I'm trembling, waiting, as I
did the other time. I see a solitary yellow drop ride along
the hair-trimmed petals of her cunt, hang for a moment
where the lips join, then fall. I catch it in my mouth, await
the next stringy drop. Yellow? I stroke harder. She pisses
all over my face, in my mouth. Now *that's* new. I swallow
it as fast as I can. I drink it, drink it, drink it, scream, gasp
for air, cum. She is cumming, screaming. She squats
down onto me, wipes her wet cunt all over my face. I lick
it, drive my tongue between the slick, hot, rubbery ridges,
then lick it all over. My arms fall back. My body goes lax.
I am resting in a tub full of pee.

I wake up, shivering, smelling of stale urine, to the
sound of a door closing.

A mosquito is buzzing about my face. I swipe at
blank air, then sit up with my back against the cold porcelain at the rear of the tub, offering my naked arms as bait.
She will come for them. They love the smell of damp skin.

64

I scan the room, pick up her shadow giantized in the light, then spot her lacelike form. She makes a few reconnaissance runs, then alights on the meaty part of my left biceps. I smack her to smithereens. There is no blood smear. She has died unfulfilled. It is after three.

Don't leave me, Aaley, please.

I can't get up.

"Well, time to get some shut-eye." I close my eyes and try to sleep.

I am Jesus with the cross again. My eyes scan the crowd of onlookers, hooting, shouting, mocking, "crucify him." My eyes meet her eyes, for an instant. For less than an instant. For a non-instant. No, it *was* for an instant. It is she, the prostitute. Oh, God. Oh, God. *Elohi, Elohi, lama shebaqtani?* Is there no depth to which I will not sink, to cling to life?

12

When I was a kid, I used to whap butterflies with weed branches, then examine their dying bodies, often disappointed that I'd torn through the designs in their wings. But, hey, I was curious, and they weren't going to hold still so I could examine them. You do what you gotta do in the name of science. Like with the Japanese beetles. But them I wanted to watch die. I used them to learn about death, putting them in jars half-filled with water and watching them stroke until they were exhausted and could stroke no more. I noted the initial frenzy when they'd taken the full measure of their situation, followed by the physical exhaustion, then what appeared to be acceptance and finally a sense of relief that the exhaustive demands of trying to say alive were finally over. I did this because, I now realize, that I'd been denied the most important death of my life.

13

The night my father died
I was born.

It made for some extraordinary birthdays. I could hardly blame my mother for being less-than-celebratory (there was so much else to blame her for.) -- especially during the early years when the day might have taken on a positive aspect. When I was old enough to appreciate my mother's feelings -- or lack thereof -- about the day, it was already too late to salvage its positive aspect. I thought about simply designating another day, but by then I really didn't give a shit about any kind of celebration of my birth. I felt there was no need to celebrate me for my birth -- I'd had nothing to do with it. On the other hand, I was not to blame for what had happened to my father, at least I didn't have any reason to believe I might have been. In any event, somehow, I couldn't get past a certain sense of guilt and my mother did nothing to ease my pain.

There were never any men in my mother's life. She had no sexual personna that I was aware of. Actually, she never gave me any reason to believe she knew my father very well. She never spoke about him, and I never had the desire to press her on it. He was a non-entity for me. I suppose I should have wondered if I'd inherited anything physiological or psychological from him -- I don't even know what he died of -- but I never spent much time thinking about it.

My mother was a librarian. She buried herself in books. She spent all day wheeling her cart between the rows of shelves: refiling, re-aligning, adjusting, dusting, ti-

dying-up; or she'd be at her desk reading; or quieting un-
ruly children.

The library was my mother's universe, one over
which she did her best to gain some measure of control, but
with which she managed only an accommodation, great by
most comparisons, but impossible to conquer in any absolute sense. She knew that somewhere along those avenues
of volumes were the answers to everything, but the answers were fragmented, compartmentalized in the limited
apartments above those avenues, defined within the confines of the spine of each binder. The formula for stitching
together all these fragments into the great design was interminably elusive. The thoroughfare defined by the aisles
and the shelves that stood on either side was only a deception.

As I grew older, I began to see my mother's role as
that of overseer, the guardian of the stacks. After years of
experience with the system, she had acquired so thorough
an understanding of location that she could direct you toward the solution you sought before you had finished your
question. When she was familiar with the subject matter --
and she had read almost everything on the shelves -- she
would even offer some very specific suggestions about
what to read. If, based upon a brief exchange, she disagreed with what she perceived to be your point of view,
she'd direct you to the strongest opposing arguments, without of course letting on what she was doing. Her actions, I
was sure, had reversed a number of strongly held positions,
but, in most cases hardened others beyond reversal.

When I was in elementary school, she'd pick me up
each afternoon and take me back to the library. There,
among the corridors of volumes, I spent my single- to early
double-digit years, fantasizing. In my dreams, the stacks
really were tall buildings, the aisles principal thorough-

fares. From a distance, the book bindings did look like windows of apartment houses and office buildings and, if I allowed my mind to wander, I could imagine just about anything going on behind those imaginary panes of glass. So, from a small desk and chair in the children's section, I daydreamed my little dramas. Women undressing and begining to do delicious things with their bodies, touching themselves the way I enjoyed touching myself, to growing effect. Then, always when things were about to get to the point where something was about to happen that I had not yet encountered or managed with my own manipulations, lights would go out in the windows and my daydreams would end. I desperately yearned for a real female to finish the fantasy for me, but I wanted one I didn't have to talk to, explain things to, answer questions for -- one who would simply do my bidding, perform what I asked.

In between these mental voyages, I read. But reading had upon me the opposite effect it had upon my mother. The more I read, the less confidence I had in the truth of what I was reading. There was no argument I could not tear down, even at a very young age. The stacks, for me, were a great repository of bullshit, written by bullshit-artists.

Each evening, when my mother brought me home to our apartment, she'd fix some unappetizing dinner and we'd eat, exchanging a minimum of words. Her reverence for the printed word did not extend to the spoken. On the printed page, words had meaning, even if she disagreed with what she determined that meaning to be. If a sentence were loosed into the air, it was ephemeral, and once its sound waves had dissipated, lost and therefore inconsequential.

After dinner, I'd head for my homework and she'd retire to her books. Always more books.

69

I hate my mother. There, I've said it. It's out in the open. I should explain why, but I have no explanation. Because I really haven't thought about why. Has she been good to me? Who the fuck knows. I could think that through, But why? There is no definition of good that anchors me. Is there an absolute definition? To me, it's aahhll relative. Who gives a fuck, anyway? I hate her; end of story. Does it really matter? In the overall scheme of things? Does it matter in even a small way? I guess it could be a minor inconvenience, but for whom? Not to me. And she doesn't give a rat's ass. Certainly not now she doesn't. Has it affected the origin or will it affect the termination of the universe? Will I have to answer for it some day? Why? You are what you are, right? I can deny I hate my mother, but it's there and denying it won't make it go away. What the fuck is hate, really? A guttoral thing. Love? Guttoral. Are hate and love different faces of the same emotion? I think yes. We have hate so we know what love is. We must have evil so we know what good is, shivers and dribbles so we know what an orgasm is, this side of the fence so we have to climb to the other side.

Can God climb a fence?
Oh, dear, - I guess if He were a Boy -
He'd - climb - if He could![1]

Why must we suffer because He can't climb a fence? Can't have an orgasm? I must be eternally grateful? Eternally? Eternal, unquestioning love? Later, Man. Non-time. Non-place. Now, here . . .

Do you have to love someone to hate them? I don't know the answer to that one. If the emotions were the same or had the same derivative, wouldn't that be so? I need to think on that one a while. Why should I feel any attachment to my mother? What, after all is said and done, is she to me? Because she is the organism that expectorated

70

me through her cunt lips, does that mean we should have some kind of emotional attachment? Because she spewed me from her guts. The night my father died. If he is dead. I don't know. I don't really know anything. Anything.

I am at my desk watching one of the windows near the far end of the stacks. Two women live there. They are horsing around, tossing pillows, taking playful swats at each other. The older one has said something that has made the younger one freeze in frame. The younger one turns and bounces the older one onto the bed and begins pulling at her clothes. A light goes on in the adjacent window. It is a bare bulb, hanging from a naked wire. The light begins to glow brighter. There is a figure silhouetted in the light, but I cannot make him out. The light brightens. It climbs over the roll of ratted window shade, spills over the windowsill. The younger woman has her roommate pinned to the bed. The older one has given up the struggle and the younger one is unbuttoning her blouse. The light from the adjacent window grows brighter. It is washing across the window where the younger woman has released the final button on her roommate's blouse. The skin beneath it is as white as the light washing over the entire building. It is stretched to near transparency. The younger woman begins pulling at the older one's skirt, but the light from the adjacent window has become so bright I can no longer see clearly. I close my eyes. Two inverted triangles drift behind the flaming red insides of my lids and float behind my light-blinded eyes.

I rise from my chair. Walk down the row. Light now is splitting through cracks in the masonry, bursting out through the roof and streaming towards Heaven. I am adjacent to the window where the light bulb hangs, but the light has gone a magnesium white. Behind it is the silhouette. He has his back toward me. The adjacent window is now

71

drowned in light. For an instant I see a small child clamped to the breast of the woman on the bed. The younger woman sees me and beckons. The child sees me looking at him, his cheeks puffed with mother's milk. He spits at me. I catch it in my right hand. It is a piece of flame. I cannot shake it. It is seering my flesh.

A man is hovering over me. He is holding a clear plastic cup over my nose and mouth.

"Breathe!" he is shouting. He slaps me alongside my face. "Breathe, God damn it!"

I take a deep breath and begin to cry.

With the library gutted, my mother lost her job. She receded into her apartment, reduced to a subsistence existence on the public dole. She'd managed to rescue seven charred volumes, which she read and re-read until she could recite them, word-for-word, but they were only words -- impermanent. Gradually, her speech left her. It was useless anyway. Then her motor functions, first her legs and finally all movement.

She lives in a nursing home. I'm not sure where. I got some correspondence early on, from a law firm trying to search out her assets, but I didn't respond and the letters stopped coming.

Whoever does not hate his . . . mother cannot be my disciple . . . whoever does not hate his father and his mother cannot be my disciple.[2]

The burning in the palm of my right hand recurs un-predictably. I live with it.

14

She slides back down my body, her hands hot against the lubrication of my sweaty skin.

"Tell me about the night your father died," she says.

"What are you talking about?"

"You talk in your sleep."

Oomieka never said anything about it.

"I don't remember anything about my father."

"Then it's bottled up in dreams."

"I never knew him. He died when I was on the way."

"You talk about him, you do."

"Well that's interesting. What do I say?"

"That's what I'm asking you."

It's a movement beyond the prevailing rhyme scheme, albeit quite elementary -- the AB/AB thing. I determine to drop the A; it makes the B more difficult.

"I never knew my father. My mother never spoke of him."

"Then where do you get what you say? You do know what occurred just now?"

I think a moment then respond, "yes."

"Tell me. About the dream."

I touch the soft flesh of her face.

"I am walking down a hall in my elementary school, headed toward a janitor's closet. From a distance, I can see a washbucket in the shadows, with a mop handle standing in it. The bucket is filled with dirty water. I can't see the water, but I know it's there and I know it's dirty. As with dreams, I am both participant and spectator. I am hesitant, but continue. I am inexorably drawn to it. I feel the need to lave myself in it, immerse myself in it. But there is something terrifying in the closet. He is there. As I cross the threshold and reach for the mop, my hand passes through an electric field. The hum intensifies the terror. I know I am doomed. I am in zero time. The terror will not go, but I see you on the outside of the dream and I call to you. And you wake me and I am saved."

"You called out: 'the night my father died.'"

"It's the title of a poem."

"Read it to me."

"I can't . . . I haven't written it yet."

"I know."

Again, I touch her face. The softness clears my fears.

"Why did you marry your wife?" she asks. She begins to move her head in small circles, no . . . ellipses.

"Because I needed her to live."

Her eyes are rolling around. I place my hands on either side of her head and constrain the oscillations. The fire in the palm of my right hand has insinuated itself into the foreground. I don't want to burn her. I stare into her eyes. The black flecks are fading into the green. The green is softening around the edges. She is frozen on something. Oomieka? A chill rivers through me. For a flash I see a side of Oomieka I did not know existed. It is what's causing the cold flash. But it is gone so quickly, I'm not even sure I saw it, or that it was even there.

She is back.

"You can't keep yourself from death."

"I like it here."

"Do you?"

I don't answer.

"One day you'll have to return and face the music."

The music.

74

Suddenly I am panicked. There will be newspapers in the driveway and I will not be there to retrieve them.

"I must go."

"She isn't home. I thought we had the day."

"I thought so, too."

There is a deep, deep sorrow in her eyes. I must escape it. I go.

15

There is a letter from Oomieka in the pile of mail behind the door. It's not like her to write. If she has something to tell me, she calls.

"I've been trying to reach you on the telephone," it begins, "but you have not been there, and I am not surprised, which, of course, is the problem . . . "

There have not been any messages on my answering machine.

". . . I will not talk to your machine, so I decided to write, because you don't get a chance to interrupt . . . "

The words frighten me. She has reached a conclusion about something. She wants something to change and there are aspects of my life I do not want to change, until I take the initiative. Is she leaving? I've never considered that possibility. I do want to interrupt. Instead, all I can do is read on.

" . . . I need a husband. The girls need a father. I could leave you, Max, and start fresh, but that would be too easy and it would be as if our lives had amounted to nothing, had stood for nothing. It was you who asked me to marry, Max. It was the two of us who created our children. It is time for you to come home, stay home, and make the second half of our lives together have some meaning. You can write your poetry, Max, create your perfect poem, but it cannot be your all-consuming passion. Your excuse for all the crap you get away with. I am your wife. You are my husband. I want you to come home. I do not want to talk to your answering machine. I want you to be there, just once, to answer the phone when I call. I am prepared to fight.

Your wife,

Oomieka"

Fight?
For what?
With whom?
This changes something.

16

The haze of sun sits like a beaded curtain upon fractured crystals. A momentary light shaft spirals earthward, exposing spectral colors, like a beam through a fish tank. Then it burns out.

I am walking along the beach a half-mile from my house. The molecular layer of moisture has settled upon my face and moistened my beard; it coats my sweater, raising follicles of synthetic fiber. For some reason, it is more disconcerting on this artificial skin. I am sweating beneath the sweater, the two layers of moisture creeping towards each other. I produce the inner film, but otherwise am irrelevant to the process. In the distance, a black dot takes the shape of a human female. She is coming towards me. The body rhythmics are familiar. It is Bags. There is no place to hide in the desolate landscape, not even in the circle of my own shadow.

Because I cannot hope to turn again
Consequently I rejoice, having to construct something
thing
Upon which to rejoice.[1]
I consider a U-turn, but time has exposed me.
Because I know that time is always time
And place is always and only place
And what is actual is actual only for one time
And only for one place . . .[2]
She has recognized my rhythm. I continue forward. My legs incorporate a nervous quake. She has read that as well.

I know what you have done.
Our Wednesdays are in ashes.

She does the U-turn, is walking beside me. We do not look at each other. We are profile to profile. We need never endure a full face. We do not speak until I break the silence.

"It's over, Ruth."

She holds her course, her silence as well.

"Try to fix it with Walter. It's what you needed to do all along."

"So you did use me, Max."

"We used each other, Ruth. It worked for both of us, but now it doesn't work --"

"You used me, Max. Save the bullshit."

"You knew it would end, Ruth."

"And now you just throw me back."

"It had to be one of us. Actually, I'm sorry it had to be me. I'd have preferred it the oth--"

"You're so full of shit, Max. You used my cunt and now you're using another."

She's right, of course, on all accounts.

"We had our moments. They worked for both of us. We knew it would end. It's time to move on."

"You'll do her the same way, Max, the one with the apartment on Hill. The young one with the pasty skin and the jet black cunt hair."

I shiver.

"But me, Max. I'm not going to disappear into the past. I'm not going back to Walter. I can't. I'm going to have to tell him."

"Tell him what, Ruth?"

I do not look at her. I cannot. We are both watching the horizon line. I can feel it. I can feel her smile.

"You know you're such a shit, Max, you selfish bastard. You don't give a shit about me. You're just worried when I tell Walter about us, he'll cut your dick off."

79

About us? What about us? Who the fuck are you anyway?

Your honor, I've never seen this woman before. She's talking nonsense. The jury finds for the plaintiff. Chop!

She is gone.

My chest is soaked in sweat. Wet fluid from an old wound. The sea is the color of effluvium. The cracked crystalline line runs to the point. The sun is burning out.

17

"I'm expecting an important call."

"That's it?"

Not all?

"I need to be here when it rings."

"At times we must do certain . . . "

Things. Things. We must do certain things.

". . . we must do what we must."

Something is broken. The rhyme, of course, but also the syncopation. Perhaps an advance to a higher plain.

When the phone rings, I ask her to leave me for a moment. She wanders down the hall. I pick up the receiver.

"The girls and I are coming home on Thursday. (It is three days off.) I want your attention when I get there."

"I have exams to prepare. You know that ties me up."

"Make the time for me."

"Oomieka, we'll talk when you get here."

"I'm serious about this."

"Why are you doing . . . whatever this is you are doing?"

"You are my husband, Max."

"And?"

She is unresponsive.

"And?" I repeat.

"We'll talk when I get there."

She hangs up. I sit in silent contemplation.

"I like this."

It is Aaley in the doorway. She is holding the poisson d'or from Cap d'Antibes.

"Where did you get that?"

81

"In a box on the dresser in your bedroom."

"It belongs to my wife."

"I know. I like it."

She is doing the eye-thing with me. But it is antagonistic. Christ, not her, too.

"Then wear it. But only for three days."

She smiles then dangles it before my eyes. I take it, kneel and attache it around her ankle. She seems pleased. My mind is swirling thoughts, but they are all in disarray.

"May I stay a moment, please?"

"With me here on my knees?"

It doesn't work this way, the B before the A.

Her smile intensifies. She raises her skirt above her waist, pulls her panties below her hips and wriggles them to the floor.

"Lick my pussy, Maxie . . . please?"

I shake my head, then do as I've been asked. It is, of course, I must admit, a not unpleasant task.

BB.

18

I am thinking of Bags and her sagging breasts. What is the attraction?

A missing tooth or a nose eaten away or a fallen womb, any misfortune that aggravates the natural homeliness of the female, seems to be regarded as an added spice, a stimulant for the jaded appetites of the male. [1]

Woman objectified.

Ruth is my carnival, my need to experience something hideous. Suddenly, I lust for her.

I am walking down Sound Beach Road heading toward the beach, the sound. The sound. Grit disturbed. He is behind me, creeping along, stopping, foraging, finding, hoarding. I call him Bottom-Feeder. A wrecked wraith of a man, with two bent rods for legs, a caldron-shaped midsection and a skull that died two thousand years ago and now is held together by a plastic baseball cap. Two lips are pasted on above and below a limp-limbed cigarette. The grey Lumina glides past me to the blue recyclables bin by the mailbox in front of the old sea pilot's mansion. The car door opens and he lurches toward the bin as if he is racing me to it.

Pay dirt. A plastic Pepsi and a glass Coors. I can feel the lips of his black soul wrinkle a smile. He adds the two dead soldiers to the green body bag on the back seat of the grey Lumina and climbs back aboard, shifts into drive and releases the brake. I hear the whistle of a cardinal in a nearby sweet gum tree. I have seen this one in his perfectly tailored red vestments, calling hypocritically to his brown-bloused mate. He wants merely to partake of her fa-

vors, then re-perch upon his limb and issue pronounce-
ments re the conduct of those of us below.

The Bottom-Feeder rolls on toward the rusted drum
by the rest rooms at the foot of the hill by the beach.
There, he leafs through spent rubbers, the remainders of
last night's carnival. Ruth is my carnival. I lust for her.

19

My relationship with Simeon Golan was tortuous from the very beginning. Simeon was imported as graduate studies chair and that put him at the top of the shit list of most of my colleagues, most of whom felt smartly slapped across their academic visages, but not me. I understood the department's general lack of administrative talent, including me, especially me, but most of my colleagues were affronted. That got Simeon off on the right foot with me. And he sensed immediately that I might be an ally, or at least not an enemy, or at the very least not a pretender to his throne, although in a very short time, he realized I could not ascend to his position even if I'd coveted it, but the initial bond, albeit weak, held.

I don't expect much of most relationships and this one did not cause me to abandon that general assessment. He protected my ass and I accepted it, played with me and I tolerated it.

He seemed to take an interest in my writing from time to time, at oddly syncopated intervals, and that pleased me, but then he would back off when it appeared the encouragement was having a positive effect on my enthusiasm for my work, especially if his encouragement appeared to be pointing me toward some new territory of theme, approach or format. I would get a sense of fear emanating from him, sometimes approaching terror, a sense that any alliance with me would cause him to share my destruction.

"You're a B poet, Max, B minus to B plus, but never A," is his current assessment. "O.K., occasionally, in brief passages, you may be A, but the mediocrity returns so quickly I lose my incentive to return and consider the best passages to see if they succeed."

Simeon, I decide, is jealous of me. I write. He critiques.

I am walking with Simeon across campus. He is on his way to a meeting -- confrontation -- with a committee which evaluates the curriculum. Simeon views the committee's efforts as an intrusion. "Nothing of value has ever come from evaluators," he says.

This is absurd. We are just fanning dead air.

"Tell me, Simeon," I respond, "what is it that's on your mind; what is it you want to tell me?"

He stops, leans one hand on an olive tree and stares at me for a moment. I get an odd sense that he is . . . evaluating me. As a man of position, Simeon has that defensive sense which allows him to sniff out any breath of disloyalty which may build to a palace coup, or, in my case, transfer my dependence, or, worse still, destroy my need for it. To pursue his agenda, he would drop me so quickly our past would be instantly nullified. But from me, for now, he needs constant reinforcement, and that establishes a value for my poetry his words deny.

"I am *with* you, Max," he says, finally. "I applaud where you are going."

"And where's that, Simeon?"

"Why the unknown," he answers, as if I should know what he is talking about.

He does that to me, Simeon does. He says things that come from some place deep down around the cornices of his bowels. He intimates that he knows about my journey and is throwing his bags on board, then grasping for the handrail, but if I evince any sense of appreciation, I see him waiving good-bye from the station. It is an odd ride.

86

"You're a piece of work, Max, I won't deny you that," he says, then leaves me flat, under the . . . tree.

20

I am on my way to see Terri Sas, my masseuse.
That's Terri as in Terrence. Terri used to be male. Still is,
as far as I am concerned. She has a live-in boyfriend and
she claims they fuck all the time. I try to picture it, but get
sidetracked in thoughts of mutual beardburn during aggressive foreplay. Norton, to hear Terri tell it, fell in love with
Terri's hands during a massage and sprouted an erection
not even Terri could overlook. Terri is blind and Norton
promised to look after her. In exchange, Terri delivers the
world's most sensational handjobs. The assessment of Norton, with the concurrence of Terri. "He's hit the fuckin'
ceiling more than once," Terri has told me more than once,
"but at seventeen inches, he's halfway there before he un-
loads."

"No one has a seventeen-inch cock," I counter. "Besides, you're blind, what the fuck do you know?"

He flexes his fingers, smiles through the half-inch
pancake makeup Norton applies every morning. "I know
you are six-point-two inches," he says wickedly.

I've almost taken a ruler to it, but somehow I know
the son- of-a-bitch is right.

Seventeen inches. I'd pay money to watch that
slide up some girl's asshole. I can't imagine a cunt that
could accommodate it all without blowing out the back
wall of her vagina.

Terri has magical hands, mystical fingers. Handjobs, why not? What else? Unless there is something to
her rhetrofitted cunt that makes a night in the sack with
Terri a truly unique experience.

"You have a knot at the base of your skull the size of a kidney."

"A knot?"

"A muscle mass. Some of your fuckin' brain dropped. You have a cranial hernia." He snickers.

"Don't get physiognomical on me," I say. "I know you learned what little you know from a rub-down flunky for club fighters."

"Physiognomical? You make that shit up because you're a fuckin' professor. It's a non-word. I know it. You know it."

I smile, but he can't see it, of course, and anyway my face is in the face hole in the massage table which accommodates your head when you are on your stomach.

"No one fights in clubs any more, Max, and you know it. I was taught by the massage therapist for a pro football team and you know that, too. You're such a bullshit artist."

"Well then, quit you're bullshitting and fix my neck."

"You're tense all over, Max. You need to simplify your life. Get rid of the old woman; keep the young one."

Ruth? Aaley? Did I tell him about either of them? Did he work me into some kind of massiacal trance and I spilled my guts?

"You're doing it again," he says, his fingers fixed on the spot, the knot.

"Doing what?"

"A non-word."

What did I say? Did I say anything? No. Nothing. This time. No time.

"Never mind," he says.

"So, smart ass, what makes a word a word and a non-word not?"

89

"The knot," he answers, "is in your neck, at the base of your non-brain."

"Oh, it's a brain, all right."

"But what good has it done you?"

"Bad. All bad."

His fingers knead my neck, begin to dissolve the pockets of tension coagulating where my brain connects with its life-support system. His undulating digital probes loose blocks of frozen meat and send them home to thaw. He presses with the ball of his hand, pushes outward as if he is working a cutlet, flattening, stretching, thinning. My face has settled comfortably into the hole in the table, the cotton covering stretched softly against my flesh, its fresh-laundered smell conjuring up sheets blowing in a spring breeze. It is almost intoxicating. I want to wrap myself in it, enshroud myself, disappear, anywhere, somewhere, no-where, nothing, nihil.

"I can't get all of it in one session," Terri Sas declares. "You wouldn't be able to hold your head up."

"So you're going to leave me in this condition?" My voice is muffled to an odd buzz against the fabric.

"What you really need is a great handjob," he says.

"Promises. Promises."

"Turn over."

"Don't fuck with me, Terri. You know I don't do boys."

"You still don't believe I have a real pussy?"

I lift my face out of the hole.

He is shaking his head. "There's only one way to settle this." He pulls back the tip of his belt, releases the tongue from its punch hole. Then he reaches for the zipper of his hospital-white ducks.

"I believe! I believe!" I roll onto my left side.

90

"Oh, have a good look, Max. It'll give you the hard-on I need to work with."

Before I can protest further, he has dropped his laundry and pushed his surgically created vulva into my face, the curlicued wires of his perfectly shaved triangle tickling my nose. It smells . . . like a cunt.

"Hormones," he says. "O.K., I cheat." He holds the hirsute patch against my face and I am thankful that at least from this perspective I can't focus on the . . . whatever it is within. But I can feel it against my face. And I can smell it. And I'm almost tempted to lick. It's a reflex with me, whenever I'm in this territory. How the fuck did they do that? Remove a real one from a real woman? Can they sign you up as a vagina donor?

Terri laughs.

"What?"

"You're getting hard, you horny bastard."

"It's one of those reflex things. Besides, how the *fuck* do you know?"

"Le'me feel?"

"No!"

"I'm right, ain't I?"

My God, It *has* leaped to enraged mode, and Terri . . . has his fingers wrapped around it. He pushes me over onto my back, without protest.

"Six-point-two," he says, "at full salute. Right about that one, too."

"Fuck!" I spurt.

"Uh-uh," he answers. "That's reserved for Norton."

I don't hit the ceiling, but it is one of my more memorable eruptions, spitting singleton boulders high into the sky, before the full flow of lava. His hands have felt like . . . I might have expected, except this was a whole new maneuver for me. He applies a non-linear progression

91

of a variety of pressures and, when he feels the veins bulge into tautened hawsers, he squeezes. The first full shot hisses against the chandelier -- it hangs a full two feet from the ceiling. The second shot hits Terri in the right cheek and hangs there in a milky thread. He tries to reach it with his tongue, but cannot. He wipes it off with one of his hand towels. "Not bad for an old fuck, Max. I didn't think you had it in you."

I am feeling odd about this. "What's this all about, Terri?"

"I don't know. I wanted to do it for you, Max."

"*For* me?"

"O.K., *to* you. I wanted to see if I was right?"

"About what?"

"About everything. I always am, you know. I see things the rest of you can't. Gift of the gods. They had to do something to compensate for this terrible affliction."

"This girl thing?"

"My blindness, you asshole."

I am in full retreat emotionally. He senses it.

"So, Max," he resumes, "your first homosexual experience?"

"You're a fucking . . . girl."

"That's what I been tellin' ya, sweetheart."

"O.K. O.K. I believe."

"Only when it serves your end."

"Oh what the fuck do you know?"

"Everything. I told you."

"You don't know shit."

"I know you've been wanting me to do this for a long time."

"Is that what you're going to plead to the authorities when I petition to have your license revoked?"

His face drains color.

92

"Oh, don't sweat it. I'd have to admit you did what you just did."

"Don't let me stop you."

I let out a sigh.

"You men always get weird on me the morning after."

I smile. He feels it.

"Still friends, Max?"

"You know I love ya . . . sweetheart."

The color is back. His dark brown eyes twinkle.

"Stop thinking of me as a he, his, him."

I study him a moment, note the look of anticipation in those deep, directionless eyes. The need for acceptance, approval burning from the surface of his skin to the roots of his hair.

"All right." I nod.

His . . . Her smile widens. He brushes a hand across my chest. His smile crashes.

"What?"

Her fingers spider across my breast, from armpit to armpit.

"I'm so sorry about Oomieka," she says.

"What? What about her?" My voice quavers concern.

She is distant, her eyes semi-circles caught beneath the lids, the flesh beneath her overdone cheeks flaccid.

"What?!" I repeat. "What do you see?"

"Not physical harm. Not to worry there . . ."

"Her work?"

"No."

"What?"

She pauses. "I'm sorry, Max, it's gone. It was there . . . now it has gone."

"Wha--"

93

"Don't bother. It's gone, completely. Without a trace. That's the way it is. Like when you've had a brainstorm but it's gone before you write it down."

"You said there was nothing physical."

"If that's what I said."

I drop it. This is nuts. I'm talking to a blind, transsexual masseuse like she was the Oracle at Delphi.

"Get up, Max," she says. "I got a five o'clock and I don't want her to catch you here with a dribbling dick."

"Thank you for reminding me."

"Oh, knock off the denial shit. You're already starting to stir again."

The son of . . . the bitch is right. I push myself up to a sitting position, avoiding any eye contact with my groin. It'll only make matters worse.

Terri Sas is in the corner fucking with her salves and ointments, trying to muffle a silly, little-girl giggle.

"Oh, shut up!" I snap, drop to my feet and reach for my clothes.

"If we do this again, I have to charge you," she says.

"Fuck you."

"Your vocabulary is contracting, Max. An experience with me does tend to be mind-altering."

I say nothing, fish my wallet from my pocket and slit open the billfold section. I consider, for a moment, giving her one of the singles instead of a twenty.

"And don't even think about short-changing me. Norton keeps the books and he's also in charge of collections."

I imagine that seventeen-incher up my ass. It's frighteningly titillating.

"Here," I say, handing her the twenty, "choke on it."

"It would have to be bigger than that."

She always gets the last word.

94

"See you next week," I say reaching for the door.
"Don't get weird on me."
"This advice from a known weirdo?"
"Yes."
I let myself out.
I'm so sorry about Oomieka.

21

The anticipated confrontation with Oomieka does not immediately materialize. She will determine the timing. I consider forcing the issue, but reject that. It will come when it comes. I cannot . . .

We are in bed. She is a reading one of her trashy novels. It is her favored form of escapism, this and afternoon soap operas, which she tapes and watches after dinner, while her hands wind her embroidery patterns and unwind from their day dipped in blood.

I have been anticipating a session since she returned home from work. There was the special suppleness to her skin when we embraced, the heated flush in her cheeks. But now I am growing drowsy, lying here studying the galaxy across the bedroom ceiling. I have been thinking about it since she came home, during dinner -- anticipatory with the thought. I wanted to tell her I was ready, but cannot expose myself to the rejection, if she is not.

I roll and face her, but she is unmoved. The light from the bedlamp illuminates her profile, rimlit in a thin orange line a micron thick. It accentuates the tiny bump halfway down her nose, like the ridge in a sheet of paper that can never be removed once it has been pressed into place. As my eyes adjust to the dark side of her face and the green cast it has taken on in the shadow, I fix on the four tiny lines that splay out from the corner of her right eye like the splines of a delicate, oriental fan, skeletonized by a sudden burst of wind. I am a few inches from her right hand where it grips the blood-red jacket of the book from the bottom, near the spine. The lizard skin of her hand and

96

wrist is patterned in liver spots. It frightens me to death, this aging of Oomieka. But at least her fingers retain their tactile potential. No one has hands like Oomieka. No one touches like Oomieka. Skin to skin, she can cause a rush of corpuscles to any point on my body, enliven sleeping nerve ends, revive those that have died. It scares the shit out of me, this aging of Oomieka.

She turns the page, uncrosses her legs beneath the bed linens, recrosses them in the opposite direction, remains in touch with the pulp of the pages. Her skin is emitting its smell. It is the sweetest smell in all the world. The earth's parfum. I inhale. I want to breathe every breath through the sublimating molecules rising from the surface of her body.

The nightgown is provocative, but I am not provoked. We've been allowed to retain some clues of Heaven: orgasm, of course. The shape of the female ass, the taste of a cunt, the smell of her skin, biceps, music, poetry, sunrise, sunset, a tree -- any tree -- a dog sleeping on your lap, laughter, some smiles, snow, circles, the feel of cotton, 72°, warm water, garden-fresh tomatoes, pineapple, potatoes, pasta, eggs, turquoise, dandelions coming through cracks in the sidewalk, the breeze, the sounds of the forest, silence, café-con-leche-colored women with green eyes, black, white, Aaley's long slender fingers, Oomieka's eyes.

She turns the page.

My lids, grown heavier, blacken the roof stars in night.

I hear the toilet flush. The light foaming up from beneath the bathroom door falls back to the rug, blows away in the sweep of the opening door. The light turns to window glow, liquid silver that settles only on curved surfaces. It caresses the outline of the human female who drifts across the room and reforms my cloth covering. She slides beside me. I roll to meet her. Her body is cool, malleable plastic. She massages the surface of my foot with the bottom of hers. I feel the dry straw of her pubis against my belly. She kisses my forehead with dry lips. The skin across my brow loosens, pulls toward her lips. I wish her to suck the skin from my head, from all my body, remove me, with finality, put me out of my misery. But that is not Oomieka's way: to do me as I need me done. It must emanate from her. We must get on with this on her terms. Follow her agenda. Nonetheless, I must force the issue. I move toward her. She holds me off. This will go where she goes. She does not give an inch. I am here for the ride.

"I want to kiss you . . . there," I say. It's something. And I love her taste.

"No," she answers. "I want you to kiss *me*," as if only designated parts of her have official standing. Anyway, it's something. And I know she *doesn't* like her taste. She does not want it on my lips. A cunt is to piss from and, on occasions such as this, to fuck. Odd. I thought it was something you ate. Silly me. I want to do this for her. Perish the thought. Perish at the thought.

There is an insect whose mating urge is so intense it can pick up one molecule of the female's scent at a distance of seven miles. I am not that sensitive. I pick up the scent about mid-way between the top of the knee and the hirsute delta. My sticky tongue locks onto the glistening ribbon of scent, radiating from the cleave in the female firmament and proceeds unflinchingly toward the source, whence lips with lips conjoin ecstatically (in the truest of Biblical readings), ignoring, of course, the pulsations of a tongue that will not behave. Ah, even the bees are envious of me for honey will make no pretense to such sweetness.

98

God, I love to eat pussy. Almost any pussy. What is the attraction? The taste? The feel of those pliable lips against mine; the way they open like tent-flaps when I run my tongue betwixt? The scent . . . of those millions of molecules clinging to pubic wires like crystal Christmas tree globes? The grinding, pulsing, uncontrollable, wringing and writhing of the feminine creature attached? These are but sensory reads, outward signs of an internal emptiness. I am driven to reconnect a loose wire in my animus, to satisfy some need deep in my soul. Or am I simply, as it would appear, the peg that plugs the hole, sucked to it by her internal emptiness? I've always viewed myself as the perpetrator -- it is a male thing -- when, in fact, it's me who well may be the perpetratee.

"Come on top of me."

See what I mean. That was what *I* wanted to do a minute before.

She reaches down for the vibrator in the drawer of her end table, and lays it alongside the pillow. We do a missionary fuck, with her holding the vibrator against her clitoris. I cum late, when she is well past her cum. She is biting her lip when I withdraw. Her hands are up as if to fight off my attack.

"I have hurt you."

"No," she answers, and nothing more. She rolls to her feet. I replace the mechanized dildo in her drawer. She goes to the bathroom to drain out my cum. I wipe myself with a tissue. It adheres to the sticky head of my penis and shreds. I peel, with delicacy, the shredded tissue.

She returns to bed. On her side.

So what is this all about? It is part of her reclamation process? It is to service her pipes? To show that she can still service mine, whether I need it or not? Whether I like it or not? The sad thing is I still love Oomieka. So what is wrong here? Why is this happening?

I get up to take a piss. The seat is still down. I sit. And wait. And wait. And wait. My bladder is sending out signals. But there's a crimp in the line somewhere. The expanding gland. Why not? I mean who could blame it? It lets two dribbles pass. An insult. I don't remember my last "stream." This afternoon, I was in the men's room at the university, standing there milking it when this block-shouldered boy took the position alongside me, hosed down the urinal, washed his hands, blew them dry. I still stood, milking it. I blew some gas. He left. I sit and wait. I sit? The female position. Female dominant? The female has had my blood tested for prostate specific antigen. It is slightly elevated. She is monitoring it semi-annually. I milk out a drop of seminal fluid. Release a weak trickle. Wipe the head of my penis. Return to bed. Oomieka gets up, again. Her turn. A demo. A cow pissing on a flat rock. She returns. Swings her left arm over my shoulder and pulls the front of her body against my back. She is warm. She is smooth. She is . . .

I pray for sleep to be mercifully quick, for I do not comprehend one iota of who I am or where it is I live. Everything is out of synch and I am powerless to recapture even where I've been, let alone where I am bound.

100

22

In the morning, I have a brief session with Simeon Golan. Some students have been complaining: my classes have become disordered; I have become mean-spirited. They want me to keep to the syllabus (if I can remember what it is . . . I have a copy somewhere, or I can borrow one from one of them). I feign a lack of knowledge of what they are concerned about, but it is a weak defense, so I tell Simeon to "have it your way." What choice do I have?

In class, I scan the faces to search out the culprits: an empty blackboard, cellophane personages. Three assume a degree of density: the business-suited boy with pretenses toward money, who is consigned to middle-classness by his lack of connections and inferior intelligence; the long-haired idiot with the sawed-off sweatshirt and the unlaced high-tops, trying to appear Negroid, making one irrelevant comment per class, with no sense of the artistic, whose family will compress his business-suited comrade by denying the vice-presidency he has struggled to achieve; the quiet girl with the long, curly hair, rubber-banded each day at not quite the same position alongside her too-wide forehead like a shredded palm tree blown down beside a slickened boulder; the . . .

"Well," I say, "where shall we begin?"

Silence. "Well then, where did we leave off?"

A near universal landscape of terror.

"Why don't you tell me what you'd like me to cover."

"Prepare us for the final," Business-Suited Boy pipes up.

"I haven't made it up yet."

The injection of increased fear that freezes his pale-brown eyes is a consolation.

"I don't feel like we're learning anything," Unlaced Sneakers chimes in now that B-S B has fired from point.

"It's the human condition," I reply. My need to destroy is rising like a thunderclap rolling up the wrought-iron bore of a blunderbuss.

Curly-Haired Girl's lips quiver. She has almost said something, is ready to join the mob. Suddenly, I am fearful. The cannon is turning. I *am* in jeopardy. *They* control *my* fate.

"Let me illustrate," I say. "Turn to the poem on page seventy-six. There is a rustle of paper. Again the scent of fear is in the air. How, they wonder, will I take my revenge?

"Will you start?" I point to Unlaced Sneakers. I don't remember his name.

He begins.

"How soon hath Time, the subtle thief of youth,
Stol'n on his wing my three and twentieth year!"

His diction is guttural. I try to imagine Milton's at twenty-three. I hear a smooth, velvety voice, playing across multiple consonants, pulling vowels a half-beat beyond the norm, then hitting the occasional glottal stop, for effect. I stop US amid line three.

"My hasting days--"

"What's happening here?"

He looks at me blankly. He'd expected I'd let him finish. Glottal stop.

"What is Milton saying?"

He reviews the text, quickly, because I am drumming my fingers on my desk amid that deadest of dead space when a student doesn't have a ready answer.

"Time has stolen his youth. He is twenty-three--"

102

"That, of course, is what the words say, but are we sure that's what he means?"

"We can never be sure what a poet means," he answers smugly.

"Give it a shot," I respond. "Get crazy. Let your mind run." It would probably trip over his unlaced sneakers.

"Well, maybe we'll learn more if we read on."

"I'd expected you'd have done that for homework."

"I did."

"OK, then let's proceed."

He tries to begin, but I cut him off again.

"We'll try someone else."

"I'd like a chance to respond," he retorts.

"I believe you've already passed that up," I counter and call on Business-Suited Boy.

"My hasting days fly on with full career,
But my late spring no bud or blossom showth."

"Stop! What do you think about that?"

I have no clue why B-S B is taking this course. He is wearing a baby-shit brown, lightweight, wool-worsted suit he got for fifty percent off at one of those men's wear warehouses. He must be dating an English major from another school.

He struggles out something about Milton's dissatisfaction with his career.

"His career?" I respond sardonically. "Well, let's just examine his resume for a moment. He has read the classics in Greek and Latin, the scripture in Hebrew and has written sonnets in the Italian vernacular that will be considered among the best in that language. Piss-water thin for a twenty-three year old, wouldn't you agree?"

"M-most of his contemporaries studied the classics in their original languages, didn't they?"

103

I'm almost impressed, until he wimps out by
openly appealing for my approval. I can't stop bullying.
"Do you think Milton was like most of his contem-
poraries?"
"I'm not sure."
"Take a stab."
"No."
"More advanced or less?"
"More."
"Then what is going on here?"
"Maybe he tells us further on."
"What, you, too? OK, where?"
"The last two lines:
All is, if I have grace to use it so,
As ever in my great task-Master's eye."
"Explain."
He's onto something, but he is over-matched.
"He is talking around us. He is talking directly to
God."
When did she get here? Why didn't I notice?
"Yes?"
"He is afraid of his earthly conquests. He is afraid
God has noticed. He is minimizing them for his contempo-
rary audience, but by delineating them, his pride shows
through the cracks, so he is appealing to God, indirectly, to
not squash him like a . . . mosquito on His biceps."
"He is feathering his nest in Heaven?"
"Yes."
"And God does not see what he is doing?"
"He is trying to con God."
"The whole poem is a con job?"
"Yes."
"He is conning his audience *and* God?"
"Yes."

"Can he do that?"

The bell had rung. They have left. She is gone. I .
. . will still be here.

23

Esteban is frothy today; his disjointed mode. He
flits about like an invisible force bowing boughs with the
stroke of his hand, only to have them snap back, albeit in
an altered state. He is a hummingbird whose presence is
felt only in the movement of blossom petals which have
failed to shield the core from A Rush of Cochineal.[1] He is
stream-of-consciousness painting. He does this when he is
blocked. When he has several paintings he cannot get to
work. So then, he rushes about from easel to easel, lifting
brushes and dabbing or stroking, all to a series of "ahs" and
"ah-hahs" that signify nothing. It is his muse working directly on the canvas; Esteban merely serving as the conduit
between parallel universes.

When he is doing this, he waves off intrusions as if
they were air-paintings whose persistent presence will in-
fuse them into the system. I keep my distance, wait and
watch him whirl. His energy will dissipate and drag him
down with it.

"So, what do you think?" he asks me when he is
ready. He means not the result but the process.

"I only do that when I'm drunk," I answer, "and
then the effort is only intelligible the next time I'm
bagged."

He is already into ignoring my opinion, dismissing
it with a limped wave of hand. Then he walks over to
"Work in Progress" and leaves me only the back of his blue
smock. "Hmmmmmm," he murmurs, the whirligig obviously leaving him with something to express to this universe from the one beyond. He dabs some rose-hued paint
on a pallet, then turns the pinched curve of a freeform into

the back of a knee. I see it now: the female thigh sharing a line with the lip of a face far greater than she. It's brilliant actually.

"Now that --" I say to his blue-backed smock, my words hung mysterious as wet paint. He turns to force a finish. "Now that . . . I like."

He fights off a smile.

I stand back and study the painting from afar. The faces, the bodies, the disjointed facial and body parts are suspended in multi-dimensions like windchimes with a visual component. It is a dirty picture, each fractured plate conveying a profoundly sexual image. But that is Esteban, high-sounding, dirty-minded.

He continues to beat back the smile, but he enjoys it when I pay attention to his work.

"Well," he pronounces, "what do you see? And, more importantly, what is the experience?"

"It's deeply personal," I say. "Besides, I thought you didn't care."

"I don't," he says, then gathers up the wet brushes to clean them.

I am returning home from The FOG. Work in Progress remains unfurled across the inside of my forehead. Across the three canvases drift the disconnected bodies and portions thereof, sucked back toward the center panel of the triptych to hint at the existence of a single all-enveloping female. A reassembly of sorts. The effect is definitely carnal. The mysterious, hinted-at, missing face wants to be more than that, or perhaps the concept is less. Less is more. More or less. But for me, for now, it does not happen. I have become conditioned to flesh. It is a powerful stimulus. It obviates the need to react in any other way.

107

24

A light rain sprinkles the campus. Angelica is approaching across the quad, briefcase looking like a rump roast in one hand, pile of beaten books pressed to her breast with the other, head down as if critiquing her footplant. Little to no chance of communication. I waiver between feigned ignorance and forced acceptance of my existence. I opt for a simple "hello" as she breezes by. She stops, turns, recognizes me, will simply, perfunctorily, return the greeting, then resume her more-meaningful encounter with herself. "Oh, Max," she says, "I need to talk to you." She holds her ground awaiting my reply, her hair frizzing to tiny coils like the restive do of an immature Medusa.

"I'm on my way to class," I return, "but yes, of course."

Her look is disappointment. "Call me, then," she says. "Don't forget."

25

A new cafe has opened a half-dozen blocks off campus: a ludicrous attempt at recycled Sixties, up-dated with café latte, beat-up dark-wood furniture, greasy burgers and warm beer in cold mugs that dribble cool sweat on oil-clothed tables, photos of James Dean, Marilyn, early Elvis, Kerouac, young Ginsberg, readings of ersatz poetry: songs of the street, the ghetto, the struggling artist bonding with drunks and skeletal women who rummage the dempsey dumpster for pork bones and clam shells with the rotting bit of muscle still attached. Weak fusion jazz plays accompaniment, counterpoint. The sound has degenerated into total chaos. I am drawn here to seek approval. No matter if I despise its counterfeit counterculture, its lack of relevance.

I am third in the evening's line-up. First is a middle-aged man who has lyricised bowel movements in syncopated grunts and rumbles. The audience laughs. It is not the reaction he seeks. Heavy.

Unlaced Sneakers is in the rear, sipping a kir, his female companion a beer. I consider a question on the final on the poem re shitting, but it would push B-S B over the edge and I don't want to rush his future.

Number two is a waif in love beads, torn jeans and leather thongs. She is pasty-faced and rouged. "I'm Melanie," she mouths with breath alone, no help from tongue or lips. Her repertoire is feminist anger, a condemnation of love not war. Her voice is arpeggio, then staccato. Occasionally, she throws her head back to reveal a set of upper teeth liberally punctuated with mercurial spots. She raises her right hand, gloved to the elbow in black, brandishing its back at the audience, the thumb outstretched and stiffened, accentuating the defiance. A familiar image. I have seen it. But where? Degas. "Cafe Singer Wearing a Glove." A weaker rendition. The young men click their fingers to indicate they have been duly sensitized. The women clap outright -- save one: the black-haired beauty with the thin, blue-veined skin.

Of course.

I begin.

"Olivia walks by night to meet me
where I wait and rest in some dark setting.
From behind any curtain she is wont to greet me,
alone again, but never once forgetting
what she has come for and
she does it well,
for she has done it many times before.
And I grow better in the lock of her arms,
the light in her eyes and
the life in her smell.

The roar of the ocean to me lies
on the smooth white path between her thighs.

She tires in her love for me,
and I hold with no regretting
when she returns to her home by the sounding sea
to return tomorrow --
same time, new setting."

Early G.C. actually written in the Sixties. Romantic. Antithetical to the concept, here.

Unlaced Sneakers is making a vain attempt to intimidate me with a stare that is forced and feeble. He determines we are equal in this setting. He is grading me. His

110

girlfriend, however, approves of my work. He is betrayed.
I return fire. A single blast, designed to cripple. His girlfriend will provide the misery.

The aftermath of victory is a brief muddle. I glance
at Aaley, for an instant. My enemy takes note. Retrieves
the lash. *Aaley. Ali. Eli. Elohi, Elohi, lama shebaqtani?*

I am blanking. The loss of words. Someone begins
tapping a utensil against a glass. Others pick it up. The
clinks grow louder. A chain is forged. My eyes find hers.
. The words renew.

"But since . . . my soul whose child . . . love is. . ."[1]
Stolen words.

"But since my soul, whose child love is,
Takes limbs of flesh, and else can nothing do,
   More subtle than the parent is
Love must not be, but take a body too,
   And therefore what thou wert, and who
      I bid love ask, and now
That it assume thy body, I allow . . . "[2]
The clinking is deafening.

Donne, she mouths, that's who.

US is searching the barren fields of his brain for the
reference he cannot find. The audience is beginning to
stomp their collective feet. US is re-energized, but the
lines have dissipated and he will not retrieve them. I will
not step down, not yet.

I announce I have one more. One more. My voice
is weakened by a barely perceptible flutter. There is the
scent of blood. Mine. Unlaced Sneakers is re-re-ener-
gized. I determine to play to his friend. It is a stratagem
whose failure is pre-determined in its conception. I opt instead for self-destruction, regain command. I turn to the
band and ask them to play background: "Nothing could be

111

finer than to be in Carolina." They look at me as if I am insane. I stare them down. They begin. I begin anew.

"Nothing could be finer
than to be in a vagina
in the moooorning.
Nothing's quite so pearly
than to slip beneath a girlie's
loosened drawwww-string

When the morning shadows
Slide behind the hill,
We rejoice we have those
ladies on the pill.

For, nothing could be finer
than to be in a vagina
in the moooorning.
Nothing could be sweeter
than to be in a chiquita
at the dawwwwning.

It's so snug inside there
in the morning chill
pressed against a thigh where
we can cop a thrill.

But while nothing could be finer
than to be in a vagina
in the moooorning,
before you get too frisky,
know proceeding may be risky
so this warrrrning.

It's a fearsome theme and
you should mind your course,
for if she's still in dreamland
she'll bite your small head off.

Ouch!

(But we'll risk it anyway because . . .)
There just ain't nothing finer
than to be in a vagina
in the mor - or - or - or - ning.
bum bum."

Agastness on the part of the men. Outrage in the
women. The Sixties waif jeers, then whistles. How Euro-
pean. The men begin to boo. The women pick up the cho-
rus. Unlaced Sneakers is in Seventh Heaven. His
girlfriend is shaking her head. Hey baby, betrayal, what
can I tell you. Live with it.
    "You don't want another song?" I cry. But the din
is overpowering now.
    I turn to the band. "Hey, fellas, take five."
    I turn back toward the audience.
    Aaley is gone. Her evening's work complete.
    I drop down off the stage, head back toward my ta-
ble, look for what was left of my drink, but it is gone. I try
to signal for the waitress, but she is ignoring me. Hey, I
guess I'm not wanted here. I head on out.

26

"She was there, wasn't she? In the audience."

"It's open to the public."

"You left with her. He saw you."

"As a matter of fact, I didn't. I left after she did."

"Moments later. Don't play word games with me, Max. You are in dangerous territory and I'm your only port in the storm."

Oh, paleeze.

He sips his piss-water coffee, leans back in his chair. The judgmental posture.

"I can't read my poems in public?"

He shakes his head and smiles. "That won't be the reason they give."

I'm getting sick of this shit; I really am. "What's going on here, Simeon? Is this professional jealousy?"

He looks at me quizzically.

"Oh," he finally sees it. "Fucking the student--"

"She's not a student."

The selective denial has the desired effect, albeit briefly: his eyebrows rise, then fall. He presses on.

"Arthur Tannenbourg is a major contributor. His son --"

"I am failing his son. He is trying to intimidate me."

"Failing him? Based on what? You have assigned no term papers, given no exams."

"He has no command of the material."

Simeon sighs theatrically. "You are bent on self-destruction, Max. And I am losing the power to save you."

Simeon powerless. All is not for naught.

114

27

There is something about the immense graveyard that draws me to it: the old headstones at odd angles stuck in the earth like teeth broken off in a hard piece of fruit; the sleeping trees with their branches like ganglia or the old, bare wire unraveled from around a nail. There is an infinity in this finite parcel, a limitless capacity to swallow our limitless dead. Women in sweats are power-walking the perimeter, improving their cardio-vascular systems in defiance of the headstones. It is first demeaning then exhilarating this certainty that I become dirt. I've long felt a kinship to the earth, a comfort in the touch of my palm against the warming strawgrass of a spring day. It is a comfort when I confront the solitary conclusion of who I am. Mixing with granules of earth provides a sense that I can hide, a grain in meadow beneath *the beautiful uncut hair of graves,*[1] another absent face in an absent crowd. The sun sits on the horizon like a rotted orange, glinting off only the newer, slick rectangles in short blips from all over the graveyard, as if the new dead are sending coded messages of affirmation or rejection. Rejection? Can I be rejected, ultimately. I think not. I think . . . not.

Esteban is agitated. A representative from the County Art Museum has been in to see him, has done Polaroids of some of his paintings and will present them to the evaluation committee. This unexpected shot at celebration has shaken his self-confidence. He likes the thought of being represented in a museum, however inconsequential. The whole process, however, has made him vulnerable. It gives him something to lose. It strips him of his independence. He admits as much to me.

115

I am a bit off center myself now. I don't know what to make of this. "But you don't paint to impress museum directors," I re-assure him. "They are impressed by your paintings after the fact."

"Who paints for a museum director?" he counters. There is a barely perceptible quaver in his voice. Holy shit. Esteban, you phoney bastard, you.

"All right," I press, "that was badly put. Let me try again. You have not gone to the audience; it has come to you."

"Ellen Barry sent him. She knows someone who knows someone."

The woman stops at nothing.

"I didn't tell her to do this," he adds.

"I know." I don't know.

He is working on the frame for the Haitian painting, the one the horrible woman brought him.

"It's not a bad painting, you know, but the frame she has chosen is all wrong," he says as he weights the edges of the canvas and places the sample matting and frame along one corner. He feels the need to shift from adjudged to judge. I am astonished. His demeanor has been the ultimate subterfuge. He had dropped from the game because he was deathly afraid to play.

"It needs to be framed properly," he continues. "Art is finite. It exists within borders of space and time."

"No," I disagree, "the artist frees the world of its limitations in space and time. 'By a few strokes,' Emerson said, the poet 'delineates, as on air, the sun, the mountain, the camp, the city, the hero, the maiden, not different from what we know them, but only lifted from the ground and afloat before the eye.'"[2]

"He was an essayist. A painter works differently."

116

"An artist is an artist, whether with words or on canvas."

"A canvas is finite. It has edges. It has borders."

"But what flows between those borders is infinite. Shit, you're the one who's always told me that."

"My frames finish the work, define the limits of the artist's work. It is why I became a framer. It is why I let no one frame my work. It is why I will sell none of my paintings without a frame."

The words ring hollow. The motivation has been fear, not confidence. "The buyer can change the frame," I say.

"Then the work is no longer mine. It is a hybrid, a bastard."

A hybrid of artist and audience.

On that note, he pauses. The museum thing has knocked his planet way out of orbit. Finally he sees. He knows I know. He admits it.

"You know, Max," he begins again, his eyes glazed over with introspection, "it's a shot at immortality. No matter how much an artist tries to work within the confines of his own universe, the real world always intercedes and it always does it with temptation. I convince myself that I paint free of corruption, but when something like this happens, I am exposed for the corrupted individual that I am."

The words are for my benefit, an obeisance to my prosecutorial role. "Hey," I say, "you're human. We're all human."

"Fine. But who defines what that humanity is? And why, for someone like me -- and you -- is there this attempt to extend our human occupation beyond our allotted period, beyond our real time?"

Real time?

I/O?

117

"We all fear death, Esteban, especially those of us who spend too much of our allotted time thinking about it."

He is positioning and repositioning the framing components. He can't get them to work. They are what they are. He can't change that. The aesthetic here really offends him. The lack of control he finds really frustrating.

"I can go one of two ways here," he says finally. "Do such a lousy job she sees the error of her ways. Or just frame it the way I would have done it."

"Why don't you just give her what she wants and take her money?"

"Then she'll never experience what could have been."

"So what? She's not worth the effort."

"This is not about her."

"I see. Again, it's a matter of your immortality."

He smiles. It is forced and weak at that. He has lost it with me. He knows it.

28

I make the call to Angelica.

She seems at a loss, skeptical even.

"I don't recall," she says, with a tone of incredulity.

"On the campus? The day it rained?"

"Rain?"

"Last Tuesday?"

A pregnant pause. "I'm sorry, Max, I don't recall."

"You said --"

"Can we do this another time," she snaps. "I'm preparing a lecture."

"Sh-sure," I wimp. "Call me."

Cunt.

29

In the pervasive gloom of a particularly rainy Monday afternoon, Terri Sas is incongruously bright. There is no mention of the additional service rendered during our previous encounter. Nor is there any discussion of what has turned her mind so gay. There is some kind of molecular soup coming to a boil in his brain and ions are zooming and pinging all around the room. He is humming as he works on the knot in my neck, a tune I do not recognize. I lay with my head in the hole and enjoy the experience. Despite the occasional shards of pain from the pressure of his fingers on the bulge at the base of my skull, the overall effect is incredibly relaxing. I want to doze. How odd. It is here, now, with Terri Sas I feel most cared-for, most secure, comfortably free of cares and concerns. His fingers press and pull, punch and penetrate the uniglobe created to contain the results of my anxieties, my unfulfilled anticipations, my failures. It is as if this organism created itself to force the connection with Terri Sas into a need-driven relationship. The charged particles in his brain are channeled now via the electron guns which are his fingers firing into the base of my skull, there entrapped . . . until what? Until, until they search out the path to my consciousness. I'm missing something here. She continues to hum, say nothing.

Images rise behind my eyes like clouds of greys from a smokey fire. I am Jesus dragging the cross through dusty streets, where the smell of burnt meat is depleting the oxygen I need to continue on toward death. The individual voices are, for the most part, collected into a garble of crowd noise. Occasionally I discern a question shouted in anger, as a taunt. Each time, I know the answer. But there is no time. And no one really wants to hear the answer. Am I content? If this is why I am here, to die, then why can't I simply get on with it? Because she is here, God-damnit, she is there. We almost made it work, then and there, but I could not hold it. I could not stop the movement. Because he controlled the movement and with it, took away the stasis. *Stormed by the heat of love, nothing could stop him, Nor heart hold back the flames within his body . . . His flushed desires were none the less unholy.*[1] I just did not comprehend the concept. And, in an instant, all was lost. The movement continues in the wrong direction, again. This time in the heat of the hot desert sun and blood spurting around rusted spikes to collect as coagulated globs of dusty mud.

"You see that?" she says.

"What?"

He pauses. "Nothing."

"Gone, again?"

"Yes."

"Too bad."

"It cleared something up for me."

"What?"

"Do'know."

I pause. "I saw it."

"I know. I sensed it."

"And . . . "

She smiles, wipes her oily hands on a hand-towel and tosses it into a bin. Swish, all air, no rim. "Time's up," she says. "Twenty bucks please."

I pay and leave.

30

I need a fix. I don't know why. I am shuddering. I need a fix.

I am on the phone with Bags.

"Well, well," she says, "to what do I owe this . . . honor?"

The pause is forced. She does not do derision well.

"I told you we needed some . . . we needed an interlude to reflect."

Take note. This is about fucking, Bags. Carnal knowledge, that's all.

"Can I see you?"

"I don't know, can you?"

O.K. The deviless will have her due. We play.

"I'm sorry. Maybe this wasn't . . . I guess you have plans for Wednesday. I'll --"

"No, Max, I don't. I've been staying home and thinking; waiting for you to call."

Thinking? Cogito ergo sum. My God.

"I'm sorry, I --"

"You're never sorry about anything, Max."

She's right. At least where she's concerned. I decide to give it up. I took a shot, but territory once you've conceded it; you've difficulty retrieving it.

"Same time. Same place," she says and disconnects.

The worm proceeds another turn.

31

The girl with the whale spout on her head is sitting opposite my desk.

"Forgive me my directness, professor," she says, "but I'm here to offer some advise."

They are the first words I've heard her utter. "Go on."

"I'm a psychology major. I thought I'd challenge myself with a class that is out of my . . . league. I'd trouble with Milton as an under-graduate. I'm sure you'll find this difficult to believe but I'm an A student."

They dole out A's these days.

"I'm listening."

"I also wanted a class which would emphasize quality versus quantity. I have more reading than I can handle in my major courses."

I am a bit disconcerted. So far it appears I have underestimated her. For a moment, I imagine us in the doggie position, but I can't draw up an image of what her ass looks like; I've never paid attention. That, of course, will change. The image fades to the reality of her stupid hairdo and her loose-fitting clothes. With a slight wave of my hand, I bid her continue.

"I read the poems over and over. They are lovely. No, really they are revealing. More than that, they are frightening. Almost terrifying."

God. Not psycho-speak.

"Milton's is a terrifying mind. I cannot hope to grasp more than the smallest piece of it, but I guess that's really all I want: a small piece."

"Perhaps you underestimate yourself." There, I've articulated that. Now, I focus on her curly wheat-shaft. She follows my eyes, tugs at the twisted rubber band that holds it, tightens away two wrinkle lines across that barren expanse of forehead.

"The Areopagitica was a disappointment to me when I read it. A piece of prose I'd expect to read in history or poly sci, until you deconstructed it. My god, I thought, did Milton really do that? Did he play with lesser minds like that?"

Deconstructed it? Did I do that? Did she recognize it as such?

"I was just going through the exercise to raise the question," I answer. "We can never really know, can we?"

"I think it's exactly what he did."

"Why don't you share your thoughts with the class?"

She diverts her eyes for the first time, I notice.

"I'm not an English major. I don't have the grounding the others have."

"Most of them are speaking because they feel it will help their grades."

She is still not looking at me. She lets a silence hang a while.

"You are intimidating, professor. I feel it would be like taking on Milton."

She is right, of course. I do seek to intimidate.

Again, she is quiet, staring at her hands folded taughtly on the book ledge in her lap.

"I'm not the one who complained about you, professor," she offers. "I wanted you to know that."

"I didn't think you were." It is a lie, of course. No, half a lie. Actually, one-third.

124

"Please," she says, "allow me a moment of pop psychology? From someone who knows just enough to be dangerous."

"Go on."

"You have an agenda that renders this class not much more than a chore for you. I guess at your station in life there are things far more important than the day-to-day. All I ask, as a student, is just help me a bit to move forward with my life, my understanding of it. I'm sure it will not take that much for you or divert you much at all from what you need to do. I am not your enemy; most of us are not."

"Your point?"

"Don't fight this class, professor. It's not worth it. You *can* destroy us. But to what end?"

It's not you assholes; I'm talking <u>around</u> you.

"Coast through this. Do what the administration wants you to do. Why make it difficult for yourself? Is it really worth it?"

Out of the mouths of babes.

"Thank you," I say, "for your thoughts. It's nice of you to be concerned. I mean that."

Her eyes brighten. There is a kind of personal beauty in their warmth. She rises, a bit stiffly. Her exit lacks a kind of insincere staging and that also I find . . . nice. Suddenly, I am horrified. She did not think me capable of this response. My God, who am I? What . . . have I become?

She is right; I am acting thoughtlessly. I determine to try what she suggests. If I can withstand fucking over Unlaced Sneakers, B-S B, et al.

125

32

The clock on the wall says six past six. It's Bags minus twenty-four. I have to run. She gets ragged if I'm late, might do something rash. Rash. An appropriate description. My headlights silhouette her in her beat-up Chevy Malibu, the smoke cloud surrounding her head, now bright white in the light. Emerging, she starts, "you're l--"

"I'll sign us in, Mrs. Jones," I croon. With her lagging two steps behind then settling into the shadows of some dank corner, I deal with the formalities with the latest desk clerk, a greasy-haired duogenarian who is distracted from his Guitar Player magazine just long enough to leer at me and give Ruth in the shadows the once-over. He disapproves of me and my choice of meat. Couple of old fucks.

I open the door into the mirror-encased room with the second-hand plastic furniture and the soiled, juice-stained bed.

I remove my jacket as Ruth intones, "martini?" She is not being friendly so much as continuing a ritual she introduced the first time we did this.

"Why not?" I answer.

She removes the bottle of pre-mix cocktail from a brown paper bag and half-fills two plastic cups. We toast and drink. One part gin, three parts vermouth.

"You know, Max --"

"Ruth," I cut in, "I'm really not in the mood to talk. It's what I do all day --"

"You --"

"I've got to take a wicked piss," I say, rising from the edge of the bed and marching straight for the bathroom. I shut the door and consider locking it but her thoughts

have already intruded. She is wondering what I have left
to hide from her. I drop my pants, fish my hair-swathed penis from beneath my jockey briefs, then stand and wait.
They also serve who stand and wait.[1] And stand and wait.
The rim of the porcelain bowl is laced in black pubic hairs,
bejeweled in tiny circles of dried amber. After an intermi-
nable delay, a half-dozen drops disturb the surface of the
water. I try to squeeze out a few more dribbles, but it
doesn't work. I focus on a string of jism, which floats on
the liquid film like a white worm risen to the surface to
catch some sun. People are such slobs. Don't they have
any consideration for the next guy? I turn from the unholy
soup and open the door. Bags is sitting on the bed, a cigarette drooping from her lower lip, her left leg V'ed to the
side, her right bent, the knee supporting her forehead. She
is picking at her pubic hair, pincering with the nails of her
thumb and forefinger.

"Lose something?" I ask.

She does not answer. Spears a few more vermin,
takes a drag on the cigarette, fits it into the groove of a ceramic ash tray, then regards me.

I have no fucking idea why I have done this. I have
no fucking idea how to get things started here. "Oh," I say,
"excuse me one more minute."

"What now?"

I return to the john, close the door, remove my
clothes. I dig around in the right-hand pocket of my wallet, a pasture I haven't entered since I transferred material
from my old wallet. The red foil packet has molded to the
round rubber ring. I tear the packet, retrieve the latex penis
glove and roll it into place, with difficulty, over my loose-
hanging member. I take a breath, then open the door.

Bags is draped back from the edge of the bed, resting on her elbows, the final inch of the cigarette sticking

127

straight out from her clenched lips. Her over-sized thighs
are like two super-highways, converging at the vanishing
point, a wooden volcano, emitting spaghettied lines of
some chemical toxin. I flash on my first sexual experience.
I am seventeen. It is the bedroom of a tenement in the His-
panic section. The condom is on my limpid penis. The
whore has rolled it on. "Your first time?" I deny it. She
smiles. She takes my cock into her mouth, begins a pulsing suction that feels as if she is drawing my intestines
from my abdominal cavity. My dizzying eyes focus on the
bureau on the opposite side of the room. On one end is a
Madonna and child; on the other a naked Barbie doll with
her legs spread. Through the open window, hymns drift
from the *iglesia* across the street. I cum before my dick
gets hard.

    "What's that?" Bags snaps rising to a sitting posi-
tion, her breasts separating and heading one each to the left
and right armpits. She dinches the cigarette.

    "You don't know?" is all I can muster.

    "Take that stupid thing off."

    "It's not stupid, Ruth. It's protection -- for the two
of us."

    "Against what, Max? We've done this before -- or
don't you remember?" Her eyes narrow. "You think I'm
diseased?"

    I say nothing.

    "Answer me," she presses. "Do you think I'm dis-
eased . . . or dirty?"

    "Look," I counter opposite increasingly angry eyes,
"let's do it right from now on."

    "Right?" Her eyes are afire. "There's nothing right
about this."

    Suddenly, I feel extremely vulnerable. She is eye-
level with my most valuable piece of plumbing. My in-

stincts tell me to back up a step, but I reason it would be showing a decisive moment of weakness to an angry bitch. I hold my ground. That is decisive.

"Get the fuck out, Max," she says. Her voice is chillingly calm, a cold blue blade. "Get out before I strike at you. And you're not worth the effort, you piece of shit."

I hold my ground, for no apparent reason, except perhaps in defiance of the piece-of-shit comment.

"Get the fuck out!" she bellows. She is going to kill me.

I stand frozen for a moment longer, then turn and retrieve my clothes. I dress as quickly as I can. I don't even take time to remove the condom. Bags is still sitting on the bed when I leave. I wonder what she'll do to fill her evening. She won't want to go home to her Walter-less house. Perhaps it's the desk clerk's big chance. He looks puzzled as I leave companionless. Perhaps he thinks I've murdered her. Perhaps I should have. She is a loose end. Extremely frazzled. Tinder dry.

33

riverrun, past Eve and Adam's, from swerve of
shore to bend of bay . . . Phall if you but will, rise you
must: and none so soon either shall the pharce for the
nunce come to a setdown secular phoenish . . .[1]

I await as the final stragglers poke to their seats. I
let my thoughts run down. I am, oddly, prepared for . . .
mediocrity. Her name is Sue Graf and she is smiling. She
is wearing her hair down. I read it as a demonstration of
approval, a sign of peace. I have found a return to the syllabus surprisingly simple.

My Milton class has settled into a run to the final.
We are on an even track. Most of the tension is gone.
Only Unlaced Sneakers is blatantly suspicious of my mo-
tives and even that works for me. He can no longer have
his complaints corroborated, so he, dragging the excess
baggage of his intellectual deficiencies, buckles down to
the poetry. He is a dull and irrelevant student and the other
members of the class are losing patience with him. B-S B
is struggling with the symbolism, oblivious to any sense of
rhythm. I get a strong sense he wishes he still had my for-
ays into the land of abstraction to blame for his anxiety. It
is very satisfying for me.

Sue Graf has become home port for me, in this defined environment. Whenever I feel myself drifting, I seek
the leeward shelter of her encouraging smile. Odd. I feel
no sexual attraction whatsoever. And I like her. I wonder
if I have ever *liked* anybody before. I am regaining full
command. The ease in work-a-day tension is having a positive effect on my writing as well, to the extent that it is less

130

fatalistic or, more accurately, less involved with the horrors of destiny.

Oomieka is pleased with the shift even she sees in my attitude. She has become less frightened with me, less concerned with what I might do from one minute to the next. But all of this rings false because of the absence of Aaley.

Where is Aaley? I need to see her, bring her at least to the forefront of my thoughts, my imaginings. The vertical line of her cunt intersects the horizontal line where her cheeks crease to form a perfect cross. X marks the spot. I drive my spike into the center of it. Feel the warm wet foam froth around it. Hardness cleaves unto (into) softness. Softness cushions the fall.

I need to see her.

I know where she lives but I never consider going there. She will come when she will come.

She does not come.

Fade to black.

"Professor?" Sue calls gently.

"Let's look at book eight, line three-seventy-nine. Sue, why don't you read for us."

She begins, in that soothing, sofa voice I have now become familiar with:

"Let not my words offend thee, Heav'nly Power,
My Maker, be propitious while I speak.
Hast thou not made me here thy substitute,
And these inferior far beneath me set? . . ."

Her voice is lulling me. Back into the swoon that so often accompanies this class for me.

The animals, two-by-two. The deficiency become obvious. A tactic. Part of the longer-term strategy.

" . . . Of fellowship I speak
Such as I seek, fit to participate

131

All rational delight, wherein the brute
Cannot be human consort; . . .
Pushed to this. Shit.
. . . What think'st thou then of mee, and this my
State,   Seem I to thee sufficiently possest
Of happiness, or not? who am alone from all
   Eternity, . . .
The comparison is ludicrous and He knows it. He
fucking <u>knows</u> it.
. . . Thou in thy secrecy although alone,
Best with thyself accompanied, seek'st not
Social communication, yet so pleas'd,
Canst raise thy Creature to what highth thou wilt
of Union or Communion, deifi'd;
I by conversing cannot these erect
From prone . . .
No shit, Sherlock. Fucking idiot.
. . . What next I bring shall please thee, be assur'd,
Thy likeness, thy fit help, thy other self,
Thy wish, exactly to thy heart's desire.
No. Nuuuooooo. Just someone to throw a football
around with.
"Thank you, Sue. So what do we have here?"
Blank verse. Blank faces.
"Is this not the basic conflict of the male-female re-
lationship? What has Adam asked for?"
An easy one. B-S B jumps in to cover: "A compan-
ion."
"Yes. What does he get?"
B-S B hangs in: "A wife."
I blank him.
He is weakened: "A mate?"
"Give me the text."
"Thy l-likeness . . . "

132

My eyes widen in disapproval.

"Thy . . . heart's desire--"

"Yes!"

It clicks for some, blanks for others. I leap into the void. "Adam wants someone to talk to. God sends him someone to . . . any takers?"

B-S B blanks out.

I search out Sue Graf.

"Love?"

"Maybe."

I scan the room. I light on a heavy-set girl, who has engaged me from time to time when the work has gotten vulgar. She knows why I am here.

"To fuck," she says.

"Could be. Thy heart's desire. Could be. But right now, what can we say about love and fuck?"

"They haven't happened yet," US contributes.

"True. But it's more profound than that." God, I love to dig him.

I've lost them. I need to bring them back.

"Sin does not exist. Lust, therefore, does not exist. Love and fuck, therefore, are one and the same. It's the first thing they do together. And it is pure. But, Satan will corrupt it and it will become lust, fuck will become fuck and God, in creating Eve, has given Satan the instrument through which to work his corruption. Adam has not asked for this. He has asked for someone to throw a football around with. God . . . has set him up."

"But why?" Sue Graf ventures.

"Now that is a question we can debate forever."

Literally.

133

34

"Oomieka?"

"Yes, Max?"

"I don't mean to interrupt your reading, but I need to talk about some things."

"I'm almost finished with this chapter," she says. "From here to here." She runs her finger down a right-hand page, then flips it over to show only a few lines on the next page. "Sure," I say. "Go ahead." *I wouldn't want to interrupt your trashy novel with something important to me.*

I push myself up, lift my pillow, place it flat against the headboard and contemplate the grey glass of the television on the other side of the room. We are reflected in a tiny golden window near the curved upper right corner of the picture tube, two cartoon characters stiffly separated in a double bed.

My wife folds down the corner of a page, snaps shut the book. "Yes, Max," she says dutifully, then her eyes energize as she reads my mood. "What is it?" she asks.

"Oomieka, you say you love me . . . "

"Yes . . . "

"Then why do I feel so insecure about it?"

"I don't know. You tell me. You've obviously given it some serious thought."

"I want the passion back in our marriage and I can't get it without your help."

"Max, no matter how you phrase it, no matter from which direction you approach it, I'm not going to do those aberrant things you want me to do."

"They're only aberrant because you view them that way. I love you. I view those kinds of things as an expression of our love."

"I'm a doctor," she says, "trust me, they're unsanitary. They're unhealthy."

That's it. End of story. *Your honor, now that we've heard from the medical expert . . .* My eyes show defeat. For a brief period, lying there while she was reading, I wondered what it would be like to have only Oomieka in my life. But, despite what she says about reclaiming me, she seems to be against that. Fulfilling my disgusting sexual needs outside the house relieves the pressure on her.

"Tell me, Oomieka, why is your sense of morality the correct one?"

"It has nothing to do with morality. I don't enjoy those things. I never will."

I never will.

"How do you know, if you haven't tried?"

"I don't want anything entering my anus, Max. I only want things exiting down there."

"It's not just that. Why do you keep bringing that up?"

"Because you do."

"I didn't, this time."

"You do by innuendo."

She's right. It is what I meant. At least as representative of what I want to have out with her.

"Oomieka," I resume, "I love you. I'd do anything for you."

"And, by extension, I should do anything for you, right?"

"That would be nice, but I'm just asking you to put back some of what you've taken away." *Like oral sex, sex from behind, etc. etc.*

135

"Forget it. Max, we've had this discussion before. It accomplishes nothing except frustrating both of us."

"So I should just shut up and let it lie?"

"It's where it ends up any way."

Right. And I go back on the street.

"Oomieka," I say finally, "do you love someone else? One of the other doctors at the hospital? Do you regret not having married your college sweetheart --"

"I didn't *have* a college sweetheart. Max, why are you doing this to yourself? Why are you doing this to *me?*"

"Do you love me?"

"Honestly?"

I say nothing.

"I loved you once. I loved who you were once. I don't know this new you. I thought it was just one more variation on the theme. But it's more than that, this time. You're going over the edge, Max. What is it? Age? The need to address your mortality? This sex sex sex, this sex all the time thing, it's behind you, Max. There *is* passion in our marriage. The passion of a couple of fifty-year-olds.

"I love you, Oomieka."

"Max, go to sleep. Your eyes are drooping."

She picks up her book, unfolds the corner, resumes her reading. I return to the fault lines in the sky above the bed, until I drift off among them, bound for God knows where.

35

Canada geese have left the shit field they've created around the water hazard at the village golf course and are gliding across the small pool with no apparent objective beyond admiring their images in the black glass surface. I am on my way to see Terri Sas. The knot in my neck is responding to therapy. It is a bit disappointing. I feel the disengagement coming. Once the connection between my head and torso has been fully restored, I return to the swoonless world without Terri Sas. It's not something that must be, it just is. Like all things.

"Hm," she mumbles curtly.

"These 'connections' are something they teach you in massage school to keep customers engaged, right?"

"Wha? Oh, yeah. Of course."

"So what is it this time?"

"Do' know."

"Real quick one, this time?"

"Unreal."

"Not here yet?"

"I guess."

His pressing, poking fingers have pelletized the knot into knotlets, now racing to find some neutral zone. It's over between us. It's what I see.

"So, tell me," I say, " . . . will I live / To great old age?"

"Only If never you come to know yourself."[1]

"How so?"

"Do' know."

"Again?"

"That's all folks."

"Get up, doc?"

"Yop."

I rise from the table and dress. She is engaged in busy work.

"May I use the men's room?" I ask, suddenly aware of one of the unpredictably strong needs to go.

She points me to it. I enter, close the door behind me, then wonder why.

I wait while I dribble and try, in vain, to miss my pants. I turn to wash my hands, splash water on my face, pull down a paper towel from the dispenser and dry, first hands, then face. My face stares back at me and holds me for a moment. Shit. . . *a body / That had no being of its own, a shade / That came, stayed, left with him..*[2]

Who the fuck am I?

Do I care?

And, if so, why do I care?

I am dust. Blood-spattered dust. Blood-globbed dust. Then dust. Right?

Does Terri Sas know? Has this been any more than a game? A conversational exchange, initiated by a blind man . . . woman, who needs to make contact verbally, regularly. I mean when we stop talking, all we hear is each other's breathing. And, to me, it is the only indication that I am alive.

I exit the bathroom and confront Terri Sas, standing four- square before me.

"Yes? . . . " I question.

He does not respond immediately. In the few seconds of silence, I listen to assure that I am still breathing, then stare at her, because I know she does not know -- for sure -- it is what I am doing. Then suddenly I feel as if I am, again, before a mirror, this time one that reflects the interior of my being. My being. Interesting expression.

138

36

"I fucked Ellen Barry."

I don't have an answer. I am ashamed for him and at the same time jealous. Secretly, I have felt she should have been more responsive to my poetry. It has the potential for a much greater reach than a single painting. I would have been far more responsive to her responsiveness. She has exaggerated features and dark, odoriferous Mediterranean skin with large, luscious breasts that drive me nuts. I imagine the pungent smell of her sex, the taste of sweat that pools in her cleavage. I would cleave unto her, oh Lord.

"The museum turned me down."

"Well that certainly is reason enough to get laid."

He is wrapping one of his framing projects, looks up.

"I'm sorry," I say.

The work he is wrapping is the Haitian painting, exactly as the woman had requested it. I think about commenting on that, but do not. I say, instead, "it doesn't matter, of course."

"Of course."

Esteban is a dead man. He will die like the rest of us. His work has been rejected by an inconsequential museum. That is the point, of course. The rejection, like the museum, is of no consequence. But Esteban is tainted now. He is fallen. He wanted it badly. I know it. Ellen Barry knew it. It was how she brought him down and now, I am sure, she will leave.

Ronald Richmann comes in. He is all excited. A small suburban gallery has accepted two of his paintings

139

for one of its exhibitions. They will be exhibited as part of a "new artists show." Ronald is very excited. It is obvious he has not heard the bad news about Esteban. It would be inappropriate to mention it now and spoil Ronald's celebration.

When he goes into the bathroom, Esteban tells me you have to pay that gallery to hang your work. "It's like renting space," he says.

I want to point out that that is in fact what Esteban does at The FOG, but again the comment would be inappropriate.

Suddenly, I am feeling very disconnected. Whatever force has held the four of us together has been weakened by Esteban's failure. With the atomic glue loosened, we are flying out from the core. I don't think I can come here any more. I no longer want Esteban to interpret one of my poems. His comments no longer ring true, but, in the final analysis, this whole association was not about him, was it?

I excuse myself on the pretext of having something to take care of.

"Where is Max going?" I hear Ronald ask as he exits the bathroom, as I exit across the threshold.

"I don't know," Esteban answers.

37

Zero time.
Aaley is back.
Like that.
Through slabs of orange and maroon, flat-faced
cats with Andy Panda ears, a cubed Christ hanging from a
cross of burnished brass, a child with eyes like a pair of
dugout canoes, twisted rusted steel rising like a reverse
flush to a spume of chipped porcelain commode, we walk,
she beside me, along sidewalks decorated with artists.
    The morning mist, which had clotted like dustballs
of white hair from a dead saint, is rising now gaseous gold
in the heating sun. The soft yellow miasma drapes around
strollers, sucks with the bent speeds of air through a Ber-
noulli tube. We push our way through the webbing to
study, here and there, works that catch our eyes.
    Here a theme of trees, mixed breeds.
    Around the trunk of a magnolia, hung with figs, is
coiled a serpent, with green-black scales crested along its
back in the teeth of a lumberjack's crosscut saw. Aaley has
stopped. She is pale as paper, rigid as a lance driven into
frozen turf. The black flecks in her eyes dissolve in green
pools, the putrid green of duck weed on the surface of a
stagnant pond. I follow the beams along rails of her vision.
The serpent wears a banker's suit, extends a hand holding a
book. It is a work of metaphysics . . . pure philosophy. . .
an epic poem . . . an accountant's ledger . . . the Bible.
"The Tree of Knowledge (Anti)." The anthropomorphic
serpent fades back into its scales. Aaley is re-sanguinated.
She moves to the next painting.

"The Tree of Life (Anti)." It is an oak tree hung with male genitalia. Around its base is the female counterpart with gleaming metal teeth in the shape of isosceles triangles. I await a second freeze frame. It does not come. I assume she accepts the artist's vision as is.

"I find it only marginally relevant," she says.

"The painting?"

She does not answer. Is deep in analyses.

"Modern art?"

"All art."

"As in *all* art?"

"Yes."

"Painting, music, literature?"

"Yes."

With this dismissal, we move on. A vendor is selling canvases, rolled, flattened, stretched. His sign reads, "We start what you finish." Alongside is a framer. "We finish what you start." We are beside a Catholic church, our lady of something or other. It is a church just old enough to be over-matched by its surroundings. One of the red-brick, minimalist variety built in the '50s, with an alabaster statue of the virgin out front, ignored by passersby. A young couple hunches into weathered leather jackets, their eyes glazed in desire. I watch as they move away down the path. The girl's ass fills her jeans perfectly. She is a young girl with a tight cunt who fucks with the suction of a fist clamped around your shaft, pushing the sperm to the head of your cock like a butcher squeezing the seasoned pork up a sausage membrane. A woman in fine green leather, trimmed in mink, over-made-up, is arguing down the price of a painting she could pay for ten times over. Aaley is searching the flow, locking onto now a man, now a woman, now a child, now a dog or cat. Each time she

142

fixes, she roots out something evil. A shiver courses through me. I need a locus. I return to art.

"Why stop at marginal?" I press. She has, after all, dismissed my life's quest as almost worthless. "Why not all the way to irrelevant?"

"If art were totally irrelevant, it would be significant," she says, pausing briefly before a collection of sculpture, singularly devoid of any recognizable or recurring form, any repeating or discernible thread.

A signifier? Or lack thereof? Which is, in effect, a signifier -- semiotically speaking of course. "I would think . . . of all of life's accouterments, you would find art the most significant, and modern art the most significant subset."

"Why would you think that?"

"Oh, just a crazy guess. We are dealing here with a form of expression, are we not? An unfettered release. You know, the sort of things that define you."

"Define me?"

"Sorry, you have no meaning. A momentary lapse."

She gives me the you-don't-have-a-fucking-clue look.

"I find art without any significance," she continues, apparently determined to drive home her point. Perhaps more determined to engage me in some sort of exchange. She seems, I am suddenly, painfully aware, to want to argue with me. "It's only function is to perpetuate its own lack of significance, to preserve the existence of the dead artist."

We are at a cross-path. To the left is a small, grassy area with a metal, tubular fence, painted black, hung in more paintings. Ultra-realism. The paintings mimic street scenes, give the impression you are looking out of windows. There is a sculpture of a black man holding a tire. It

143

is so lifelike I want to touch it, talk to it. Hanging over the top rail of the tubular fence is a used condom. I study it momentarily, cannot be sure.

To the right, a grouping of vendors is selling crafts from blankets spread on the sidewalk, or folding wooden boxes, opened on stands. It is the cheap shit that follows any kind of outdoor exhibit or street fair.

Dead ahead is a hotdog vendor. I opt for an infusion of murdered meat. Aaley orders only a soft drink. I have a dog covered in everything. It tastes a bit putrid. I am having a problem lately with meat.

Despite art's lack of significance and its only marginal relevance, it has nonetheless turned Aaley introspective. She is doing the woman thing, reevaluating something *significant* which will impact upon me. She is going to change directions on me. She is doing the woman thing. I walk her away from the hot dog vendor, to a bench. I sit. She is reluctant to join me, stands one foot on the bench, sucking liquid through a straw. I look up at her. She is haloed now in the misty air.

"You don't see it yet, do you?" she asks.

Oh Christ. "Since I have no idea what you are talking about. . .?"

"This is not about talking."

"This is about . . . ?"

Fucking.

"Fucking."

Oh God, we're talking about --

" . . . "

Finally, it is the morning after. It is all the mornings after I've thus far managed to avoid with her. Im-affixes to the previous perfection. I'd had it; now it is gone. Im as in not, as in less than. Not as in I'm. I am . . . now lost, predictably, in the talk about relationships, the larger

144

meaning of what we've done, the longer-term commitments established, broken, etc. etc. I don't believe this shit. Not with Aaley. Aaley *was* different.

"I fucked you, Aaley." I opt for offense. "I loved it. I thought you did, too."

The eye thing. Forest green. A grove of mid-summer fruit trees -- borrowed from an insignificant painting -- along a ridge line, black now against the orange-red of a polluted sky.

"Loved?" she questions. "I pissed all over you, Max. Literally. You drank it down."

"I love the way you . . . taste."

"Love?"

"Yeah . . . love." *Sex and rock 'n roll.*

"You really don't understand the meaning of the word, do you?"

"There is no meaning, Aaley. Right?"

"It's transcendent, Max."

"Ah, word games, again. Sans rhyme."

"Or reason."

"Jesus, we really are into the bullshit now, aren't we?"

"Love has been taken, Max. Commandeered. The orgasm has been perverted."

"Perverted? Define perverted."

"You're a pervert, Max."

"Horseshit! *I* fucked *you* up the ass, Aaley. You just about begged me to."

"It was what you wanted."

I spit a laugh. "And you did it because *I* wanted to?" I've wiped a smear of onions and red sauce across my cheek. I remove a handkerchief and transfer the blot to a bloody stain on the cloth.

"Yes," she says.

145

"You do whatever I want?"

"I did, Max, yes."

"And now?"

" . . . "

"And now?"

" . . . "

"And now?"

"Now . . . we move on."

"To where?"

"We'll find out."

"You don't have it charted?"

She doesn't answer.

"How disappointing."

Her interest in the conversation is waning. She is drifting away. I get up. We walk back to the heart of the exhibit. Now she is studying a series of wild animals in cages. Straight realism. The animals -- leopards, tigers, lions, birds, serpents, primates, a pink swan -- the eyes of each are telling. Some crushingly sad, others crazed beyond the outer borders of madness. Amid perhaps two dozen similar canvases, is one of a lone rose, pink on a misty morning. There is the hint of a castle in the background. The otherwise dominant human presence subordinated to the rose.

"I'm not going to enjoy this, Aaley. You're not the person I once knew."

"Yes."

"'Yes,' you are? Or 'yes,' you aren't?"

"Yes."

We had plateaued. We are on the move again. But I do not know if it is up or down. I do not know *where* is up and where is down."

In a shaft of sunlight by a lamp post a small group of teenagers clusters in a loose circle. Their look is radical:

146

black leather -- jackets, pants and boots; spiked hair, some in rainbow colors; earrings, nose rings. One boy keeps a tight reign on a mean-looking doberman with a studded, black leather collar. Their toughness is a bit too stylized. They are the children of the artists, taking a generational step beyond. A young woman has broken free. She is a misplaced person. She wears black leather, but it is fashionable as opposed to demonstrative. A gold chain, "Mary Beth," decorates her neck. Three rings climb the ridges of each ear, but they are evenly spaced and carefully selected. A black beret is pulled down to the tops of her ears; shiny brunette hair curls below the back of the cap. She is in conflict: to belong, to hang in, to hang out, versus a need to return, to rejoin -- to regress. She is adrift, vulnerable. She is zigging the path in our general direction. Aaley is a stride ahead of me. The young girl is twenty yards and closing. She is head down, overly intent on her foot placement. I get only the back of Aaley's head, but I am square to the young girl's face. She lifts it. It relaxes, loses a bit of its intentness, softens into a relieved acceptance. She nods at Aaley, but I sense they have never met. She reverses her field, walks with us. As we pass her friends, the boy holding the doberman surveys us menacingly. He sneers at me, something about a one-for-one trade, but he cannot pull off the act. We ignore him and walk on with our quarry. We are clear. No one follows.

We walk on. No words are exchanged. No gestures that might convey feelings, pose questions, search answers. There is no eye contact. She is part of our universe now.

We have traveled a dozen blocks when we turn right onto Hill and walk the row houses to the one where Aaley lives. The young girl turns to mount the stone steps a step ahead of Aaley. I lag two steps behind, watching the

147

girl's hips rise and fall, move from side to side, as she ascends. This is some sort of homing process. I, like the young girl, am a captive. Control emanates from elsewhere. This is ritualistic. I am a pawn. It is exciting as Hell.

"You can stop this at any time," Aaley says to me as we close the door and stand, the three of us, in the foyer.

"Do you *know* each other?" I respond.

The girl says nothing.

Aaley says, "no."

She awaits an additional response from me.

I am deadpan.

She motions us toward the bedroom.

The girl leads the way. Again, the feral movement of her febrile hips. How old is this child? She seems maybe fourteen, fifteen.

We enter Aaley's bedroom. She turns on the low-wattage lamp on the night table. The room turns a warm orange; brown shadows describe geometric shapes on the walls. The girl proceeds to the far corner by the window and, with her back to me, she slips her jacket off her shoulders and drops it on the floor near the head of the bed. She turns, looks me full in the face for an instant, then drops her chin, lowering her eyes and assumes a supplicant's pose. I move around toward the foot of the bed. The heat emanating from the young girl is sucking all the warmth from my body. A chill is rising from beneath my feet, coursing up my body in a capillary action that leaves me in shivers. The girl sweeps the black wool beret from her head, shakes her hair free. Single strands repel electrically from the black wool sweater that covers her upper body, the sweater is porcupined with stiff-standing cilia. She sits on the far side of the bed, now with her back to me again, and removes her boots. I cannot take my eyes from her. I am trembling noticeably now. My body is ice.

Aaley cuts between me and the bed, pushes me into the armchair in the corner, goes to the girl, who, with Aaley's approach, stops undressing, drops her hands into her lap and stares at her feet again awaiting guidance. Aaley sits alongside and strokes her hair. The girl looks up at her, as a nun looks to the Madonna. Aaley kisses her on the forehead, then reaches down to the bottom edge of the girl's sweater and begins to work it up her chest. The girl raises her arms over her head and Aaley pulls the sweater off, exposing a slim, youthful torso, banded in a stark white brassiere. Aaley drops the sweater near the headboard. The girl twists her back toward Aaley, who unhooks her brassiere. The girl bends forward and lets the brassiere slide down her arms to her wrists, where Aaley removes it and drops it near the sweater. The girl is profile to me. I can see her right breast, dimly rimlit. It is small, perhaps a handful, appears dense as wet clay, and rises to a nipple that looks like the conical swirl of a cream topping on a vanilla sundae.

Aaley drapes her left arm around the girl's naked back, and with her right hand pressed against the girl's breastbone, pushes her to the bed. She turns her ninety degrees, lengthwise on the bed, then loosens the zipper at the side of the girl's black leather mini-skirt. The girl rises her buttocks and Aaley removes the skirt. She adds it to the pile by the headboard. There is a bulge at the inverted apex of her panties. Aaley removes them, along with the sanitary pad that is affixed to them. It is saturated in blood, bright red. The sight stiffens me. Aaley is unaffected. With the skill of a nurse re-making a bed with the patient in it, she pulls the bed-coverings down and drops them over the footboard.

149

The girl has drawn her legs up. They are bent with her knees tight together. Still I can see the youthful slit of her cunt, through the space between her calves. It is trimmed in a soft-looking swath of brown hair, some of it matted in dried blood. Aaley places a hand on each of her knees and parts her legs. Drops of blood have already created a small red circle on the sheet.

Aaley, begins stroking the girl's forehead with her right hand, then, with her left, strokes, with feathered touches, over the girl's chest. The small, tight, beige nipples harden into blunt points, dotted with the white tips of the areolae rings. Aaley slides her hand down to the girl's vulva. She massages it around the pubic bone. She runs her index finger lengthwise between the cunt lips, then lifts the blood-streaked finger into the lamplight.

Aaley turns toward me, fixes me in her stare. I rise, undress, move to the foot of the bed. I am cold as the dead, ice blue, quaking. Aaley takes my cock in her bloodied left hand, strokes it and pulls me toward the young girl's body, trembling now, in anticipation . . . or cold, like me. I free myself from Aaley's grasp, kneel onto the bed and move toward the girl's abdomen. Aaley, continuing to stroke the girl's forehead, takes my cock in her left hand again and rubs it against the outer lips of the girl's cunt. Her flesh is warm. Wonderfully warm. A fragile moan, stutters across the girl's lips. Aaley works my cock within the lips. The hymen stops it. Shit. I am paralyzed.

"God damn it, push," Aaley says.

I begin to apply pressure. The girl begins to squirm. I ease up.

"Push," Aaley repeats.

I re-apply the pressure. The girl begins to squirm again, writhing her hips.

"Push!" Aaley commands.

150

I drop onto my elbows, drive my cock forward. A flush of heat consumes me. Melts all the ice.

I feel the membrane tear.

The girl screams.

I drive the full length of my cock into her.

She squeals.

I ease the pressure, rise back up onto my knees, pull back about halfway. I look down. My cock is painted red. The circle of blood on the sheet has grown to the width of the girl's hips.

The girl is whimpering.

"Go," Aaley says.

I begin to stroke. The young cunt around my shaft is tight and a searing fit, despite the quantity of liquid pouring out of the cavity. The girl is whimpering incessantly, punctuated by irregular squeals during inbound strokes. I continue stroking, but my orgasm is still far off.

The girl begins a staccato of "ow-ow-ow-ow."

"Go," Aaley commands. "Go!" She has a hand on my ass regulating the movements.

She increases the frequency.

"Ow-ow-ow-ow," the girl repeats. "Ooooooh."

I am still a ways off, but I can feel the sap beginning to rise.

"Ow-ow-owowowowow." The girl is crying now. Tears are streaming down her cheeks.

"Go! God damn it!" Aaley shouts.

I feel the orgasm fire up the shaft. I drive deep into the young girl's innards, and drop my weight onto her chest. She is burning, wet with sweat, beat red with heat. She smells like burnt flesh.

"Aaaaagh!" she screams.

I fire inside her. With each pulsing ejaculation, she screams.

151

And then, I am spent.

My face is against the pillow alongside the right side of her face. She is gazing straight up at the ceiling, her eyes glass, her hair wet as dishwater. I cannot focus from so close, but I can see the lamplight glistening on her wet cheeks. She has settled into a steady whimpering. I kiss her wet cheek.

"No," she cries, and turns her face away from me.

I push up on stiffened arms. With one swift pull, I withdraw.

The girl screams.

A milky globe of cum, sits at the opening of my cock, swirled with tiny oceans of blood.

I am on my knees between her legs.

Aaley is still seated alongside. I look at her. She has affixed me in her gaze again. I try to rise, but my legs will not move. I look to Aaley for help. She keeps me fixed and wriggling, but I am unable to rise. Aaley sweeps her gaze from my eyes to the girl's bloodied crotch.

No.

I try to shake my head. But nothing happens.

She turns to me again. I am stone.

She has driven the shafts into my brain.

I blink. Nod. My muscular coordination returns.

I drop my head between the young girl's legs. The sheet is sopping wet with blood.

I begin licking the girl's cunt. The taste of the blood is sweet and over-powering. I run my tongue along the ridges of the young vulva until I find the tiny, stiffening clitoris. I stroke it with my tongue. The girl begins to moan. I stoke faster. She arches her hips, drives her pubis hard against my face. I alternate the strokes with the press of my tongue against her clitoris. She is writhing her hips with greater intensity. She is moaning and squealing alternately. The two meld into a stutter. Then with a thrust she pushes her cunt hard against my mouth and cries out. With a tightening of her abdomen, she expels a thick soup of jism and blood into my mouth. It slides over my tongue and slips down the back of my throat. I swallow. Drop face down into the puddle of blood. A tiny, residual spore rests on my tongue. I can feel it moving. It is frantic to get somewhere . . . safe. To find a place to hide. I bend my tongue, push the microbe between my teeth, bite down with all my strength. The silent scream, splits my brain.

A foul smell has invaded the room like the fetid fumes off a polluted river. I await the breeze in the angel's wake, but it does not materialize.[1]

Aaley sits, rocking on the very edge of the easy chair. She is moaning an oo-la-loo-may[2] like the groan of a dead and weightless breath in the hold of a defeated warship.

She has come here to be with me. Or, I have taken her here with me. But, there is no question she is here; the evidence is clear on that point. No question.

The room goes black.

38

I am at a table in The Crucible, a club three blocks from her apartment on Hill. My crotch is on fire. My lips are swollen and chafed. My head is throbbing, violently. I am having a scotch. Neat. I am picking at a plate of nachos, cooling and coagulating on the table before me. They are covered in bits of beef, tiny cylindrical cuts of scallion and smothered in Monetary jack. The beef bits taste rancid to me. I fish around for beefless dough chips, battle the nausea, rising inside my G.I. track.

At a table to my right, on the far side of the room, near the front window, sits a lone woman, middle-aged, sipping a glass of amber liquid and smoking a cigarette down to the filter. She is wearing a black beret pulled down to her ears, a black leather jacket, and a black sweater of a cashmere-like softness that looks as if it were once expensive. The empty chair opposite is meaningless. No one is coming. I am watching her, staring at her, trying the mindmeld thing, delivering an invitation. It is a ridiculous maneuver, but all I can muster.

The woman, turns slowly, looks back to me.
HURRY UP PLEASE ITS TIME[1]
I smile. The acid inside me rises to my esophagus.

The woman extinguishes the few shards of tobacco that remain aglow at the end of her cigarette, rises from her seat, removes her handbag from the back of her chair and slings it over her shoulder. Carrying her glass, she approaches. She is familiar to me. A local barfly. I've seen her around. She is an inch thick in make-up, wears hoop earrings big enough for a tiger to jump through and a neck chain terminating in a cheap-looking locket caught on a

pull in her sweater. The mid-thigh, black leather skirt is
too tight for her ever-widening hips.

HURRY UP PLEASE ITS TIME

"I know you," she says, "you're the poet."

"Yes," I say. "May I buy you a drink?"

"No thanks," she says, "I can't even finish this one."

With a sweep of her arm, she throws the remains of
her drink in my face. The ice cubes smack against my forehead, then hit the table and fall to the floor.

"Have a good evening," I say to her back as she
sways toward the door.

HURRY UP PLEASE ITS TIME
HURRY UP PLEASE ITS TIME

The nausea erupts. I spit a spume of vomit across
the table in front of me. It is a clot of blood, jism and the
brown, green and yellow bits of food, I had ingested in a fu-
tile attempt to nourish my corrupted insides. I am bent in
half, slide from my chair to the floor. I curl into the fetal
position. The vile liquid crawls to the edge of the table and
drips onto my face. I slide under the table, reach for the
center post and grope for the bottom. I find it and hang on.

HURRY UP PLEASE ITS TIME

I'm not sure how I got home.

A Violation

How must it feel
to be on the receiving end of my attack,
to feel the heat of the invisible, pulsing
circles, emitting from my mind,
hum over you in waves of static
through your thoughts?

155

I know it is a violation but
I cannot care.
It is the way it is or
at least can be.
Mine is an attack upon your surreality,
immortal for not real.

Though you know I am
attacking, though you feel
the electric hum,
you are powerless to stop
it and incapable of running
anywhere I cannot send the waves to find you.
I know this
and would stop
if I could want to
but I don't,
for there is always
the possibility,
however remote,
that you will rise and walk
toward me
and ask if you might sit down
and not
throw the rest of your drink
in my face.

HURRY UP PLEASE ITS TIME

39

"You give no credit to the influence of your mother? There is no other influential force in your life but yourself?"

My face in the hole, I make only a muttered reply with some unintelligible syllables I hope to be mistaken for words.

"Who, Max, do you think you are? God?"

More nonsensical phrasing. Perhaps the start of a new language.

I am the light which is above all. It is I who am the all. There is none apart from me. [1]

My mother? What could she possibly contribute? Book- knowledge? An unintelligible jumble of useless facts? Besides, where would I even find her to ask?

Any one of the perished dead you allow to come up to the blood will give you a true answer . . . [2]

She is dead?

Come. Drink.

I've said it before and I will say it again . . . You are wrong Samael. . . You are wrong god of the blind. [3]

"Then she is dead."

"Of course."

40

In the road before me lies a brown-and-white hair-ball. As I approach, I can see it is a dead squirrel. Soon, under the wheels of passing vehicles, it will be ground meat, crushed guts and matted fur. I stand astride it and move it toward the road shoulder, with the side of my foot. It goes into spasm. It rolls down the slight incline where I've pushed it into a tiny ditch carved by rainwater. It is on its right side, its left eye open now, staring at me, terrified; one of the deadly giants hovers over it.

I turn away, run home, rummage through the base-ment, return with a cardboard box, an old towel and a plas-tic dustbin. I shovel the squirrel into the box, cover it with the ratty towel. I bring it home and place it in the tool shed. I call the local vet. He gives me a number for a vol-unteer group that tends to injured wildlife. I call, but no one answers. I leave my name and number on the tele-phone tape. I check the squirrel. Its breathing is shallow. A viscous yellow fluid drips from its mouth, a furry two-toothed slit that looks like a Disney cartoon face. It spasms periodically.

Four hours later, one of the volunteers returns my call. I must take the squirrel to them. They are an hour away. I carry the box to my Z, place it on the passenger seat, and drive. Once, along the way, I hear the claws scratching against the cardboard, then the scratching stops and I don't hear it any more. I am sure the squirrel is dead, but I don't even consider checking, or turning back. At the small animal shelter, a young woman tells me it doesn't look good. She takes the squirrel into a back room, returns a few minutes later.

"She's gone," she tells me. "Severe head trauma. There was nothing that could be done. It was a young female, but she was not lactating. No babies," she explains needlessly. "Now, if you'll excuse me, I have a very sick bird to see to."

Life is nasty brutish, and -- if we are lucky -- short. On the drive home, I begin to cry. I'm not sure why.

41

"Why did I cry?"

"Yours is a shaken faith, Max. You are examining, seriously, for the first time, the common plight of pain and death."

I am a greased pig, face down in the hole. "There was nothing there to shake."

"Bullshit. What do you think is going on in your poetry?"

"Tell me, Terri, do."

"You're workin' it out, asshole. It's what we're all doing in our own separate ways."

"Adherence to a faith," I counter, "belief in a philosophy, crumbles beneath the wheel of the real."

"Reality? You're not going to attempt to define that, are you?"

"Why not?"

"Because it is amorphous by definition, changeable, inconsistent."

"My point, exactly."

"Ah, Max, Max. I'm surprised. Intelligent guy like you. Faith -- O.K., a philosophy -- is not defeated by momentary disruptions along the way. Look at the Jobian model. The failures and frustrations along the way did not distort the final outcome."

"Fuck if it didn't. God wiped out that fucker's entire family."

"God?"

"Who else? God got suckered into the bet, then he relished the idea of it."

"But his justice prevailed."

"Justice? All that prevailed was his power. He over- matched his disciple, bullied his acquiescence."

"You're misinterpreting the source of the evil. It was external."

I push myself out of the face hole and up onto my elbows. "Just fuckin' massage my neck, O.K.?" I say.

He doesn't listen. No one *ever* listens. "So, what are you saying, Max? Our decisions are motivated internally, and we must let them out?"

If you bring forth what is within you, what you bring forth will save you. If you do not . . . it will destroy you.

" . . . Yes."

"So, God was workin' it out *Him*self when he had all that shit done to Job?"

He has turned it around on me.

"Yes."

I plop my head back into the hole. "If you bring forth what is within . . . My words vibrate the shroud. " . . . It will save you."

"Yes."

What next?
What happens next?
Where to from here? I fear . . .
I fear.
She was there.
Yeah,
in the dust of a hot dry
city street, doing the eye
thing. The I thing.
But she was there,
not nowhere,
there.
And it stopped me.

161

Momentarily.
A choice I hadn't bargained for.
No more.
No less.
Unblessed.
Abandonment?
Renunciation?
I hesitate.
Too late.
Damned if you do.
Damned that you do.
But now, I'm here,
in the air,
on my way home.
Alone.
And . . . I still don't know . . .whether or where . . .
I want to run,
as I have always done,
from my anxiety.
But that's just me
. . . just me.
Why?
Why do I doubt?
Why am I not sure?
Why have I been left to my own devices . . . ?
Why? Why? Why?
You doubt?
. . . You were workin' it out?
You doubt.
The mission was mine. I'd asked for it. Thus I em-
bold'n'd spake . . . Thus far to try thee . . . I was pleas'd
. . . To see how thou couldst judge of fit and meet[2] . . . *I in-*
sisted upon it. To demonstrate my strength. My worthi-
ness. An experiment that failed. With the predictable

162

consequences, like the death of the innocents in the flood. Apres moi, le deluge.

Damn the poets to hell. It was all a matter of timing.

There is no time.

Before Abram was, I am.[3]

Damn.

"It was nothing."

"Nothing?"

"You know . . . nothing."

As in zero. The sphere. The point. The mathematical problem which is its own solution.

I am full of confusion; therefore see thou mine affliction.[4]

42

Oomieka comes to bed in faded green hospital scrubs. I've asked her to wear her nightgowns, but she says she is more comfortable in the scrubs. They look like a set of grubby pajamas. I like the nightgowns because she is naked beneath them and they ride up on her body during the night, exposing her lower half. Then I can feel her naked smoothness against my nakedness. She gets upset because she is sometimes awakened by my hard-on pressing against her, trying to poke holes where there are none.

I've asked her to wear the nightgowns for me. I've promised not to press my erection against her. She has said, "we'll see," but when she says that she is just buying time until I forget about it. I have not forgotten about it. I need her to go back to wearing nightgowns, now more than ever.

Please, Oomieka, wear the nightgowns, the beautiful nightgowns. Oomieka, please?

43

"Terri?"

"Yeah, Max?"

"Seriously --"

"Uh-oh."

"Which is it now: male or female?"

"Which is what?"

"You."

He releases the grip on the back of my neck. "You still can't get past that hand-job thing, can you . . . baby?" He runs his hand up the inside of my right thigh.

I arch up like the elbow in a culvert. "Fuck!"

He peels off short of the external plumbing. "Fucking is for Norton. I told you. No matter how much you beg."

I settle back into my hole. "You didn't answer the question."

"Take your pick," she quips. "I'm either. Neither. Both."

"You low life."

"Quite the contrary. I believe that makes me a higher form of life."

"Yeah, right."

When you make the male and the female one and the same, then you will enter.[1]

44

Oomieka has the results of the blood test she insists I take semi-annually ever since it first revealed an elevation in the antigen that telegraphs prostate cancer.

"You're four-point-two," she declares.

"Great!" I exclaim.

"Why great? You're above normal."

"By point-two. And, I'm down from the five-point-one I was last time."

"Doctor Millstein doesn't like the swings."

"I'm swinging downward."

"You're erratic."

I sense I'm glaring now. She is moving to didactic mode.

"You want him to poke me, don't you?"

"I want to know definitively."

"And the biopsies will do that?"

"Yes."

"Once and for all?"

She shakes her head. "Nothing lasts forever."

"And then what?"

"The blood tests."

"Like now."

"I'll feel more confident in the results."

I shake my head.

She makes the appointment.

45

"Why do you treat your children so badly? Are you aware of their pain?"

"I don't pay much attention."

"What iniquity has been theirs to pardon?" she counters. "Are they worms? Are they maggots? Or are they your children?"[1]

I am dumbstruck. A strange sense of tenderness descends upon me. A sensation hitherto unknown. I am, at the same time, acutely aware of my ability to have inflicted pain, without any sense of remorse. The tenderness metamorphoses into deep sorrow. "What can I do?" I ask.

"Only you can answer that," he responds.

It is too late. Too late for my family. I am who I am and they are who they are.

46

I am not me. I don't know who I am, but I am not as previously defined. The disorientation follows me to my Milton class.

I am romping all over the text. Long poems, short, prose ... settling into PL, but rough-riding that all over the place:

"... justify the ways of God to men. Imagine the pair of balls on this guy. Justify the ways of God to men? . . . To do aught good never will be our task, But ever to do ill our sole delight (*Shit!*) . . . Better to reign in Hell than to serve in Heav'n . . . for whence, / But from the Author of all ill could Spring / So deep a malice, to confound the race / Of mankind . . . Chaos . . . The Womb of nature and perhaps her Grave . . . Sufficient to have stood, though free to fall . . . had serv'd necessity, / Not mee . . . thy Humiliation shall exalt (*?*). . . To visit oft this new Creation round; / Unspeakable desire to see, and know / All these his wondrous works, but chiefly Man . . . Oh Sun, to tell thee how I hate thy beams / That bring to my remembrance from what state / I fell, how glorious once above thy Sphere . . . What next I bring thee shall please thee . . . thy wish, exactly to thy heart's desire . . . Two of far nobler shape erect and tall, / Godlike erect, with native Honor clad / In naked Majesty seem'd Lords of all, And worthy seem'd for in thir looks Divine / The image of thir glorious Maker shone . . . know to know no more . . . Your bodies may at last turn all to spirit . . . If ye be found obedient, and retain / Unalterably firm his love entire . . . With envy against the Son of God, that day / Honor'd by his great Father, and proclaim'd / *Messiah* King anointed, could not bear / Through pride that sight, and thought himself impair'd. / Deep malice then conceiving and disdain (Book V, Line *666*) . . . (Jump to Paradise Regained) Also it is written, / Tempt not the Lord thy God; he said and stood. / But Satan smitten with amazement fell[1] . . . *(Shit, the son-of-a-bitch was talking directly to the father. He was going around. That exercise in the desert was pure deception. I'd read it as an attempt to tempt, but that was a card trick, the supreme deception. He was going around, talking directly to the father. He was saying get this amateur out of the middle, let's you and me square off. I don't remember reading it that way. This is a bolt out of the blue. Did the bastard make his point? Did he?)*

"Professor?"

Sue Graf is trying to nudge me back to the real world. This time, she is not up to the task. I am babbling. I gaze around the room. The class is in a tizzy. From the look on his face, Unlaced Sneakers has performed the mental equivalent of throwing up his hands. B-S B is completely adrift.

I look at Sue. Her eyes are pleading with me to save myself.

"Does anyone have any comments?" I muster.

There is silence that marks a class in a state of confusion.

"Does anyone have any comments on anything?"

Silence.

"Well then I guess we can call it a class. I'll see you next time."

There is a tentative shuffling of books and bags. One or two rise to their feet. The rest follow. They drift out. Sue is lingering.

"Professor?" she says.

169

"Not now, Sue. I've got to think something through."

She is deflated. She shakes her head and drifts toward the door. She is tentative, delaying, hoping I will call her back. I do not. She leaves. There was forty-five minutes of class time left.

To do aught good never will be our task, / But ever to do ill our sole delight.[1]

He took it. He fuckin' commandeered it. The connection. He commandeered the fucking connection.

The connection.

Aaley?

I am your connection.

Aaley has come to take it back.

?

47

A young female technician from India or Pakistan or Bangladesh prepares to do the ultra-sound with a pair of probes that could serve as moderate-sized dildos. I am on my left side, in the fetal position, facing the wall, trying to concentrate on the tiny, grey boxes that form the pattern of the rag-cloth wallpaper. She inserts the probes in my rectum and roots around in there, mumbling and hmmming. Despite the ominously predictive implications of the sounds she is emitting, the overall effect is not unpleasant. I feel the tip of my penis wetten. To kill the mood, I ask her about the biopsies. She says the doctor usually takes six to eight, from "suspicious areas."

"Are there any . . . suspicious areas?"

"The doctor will discuss that with you."

I don't like Millstein. He is young, handsome, pleasant, articulate and has an acceptable bedside manner.

"You'll feel first a pinch," he says, "then a little snip."

He begins. "There's the pinch. It feels more like a puncture from an ice pick. "There's the snip." The machine makes a sound like a stapler. I feel a soft hand on my ankle.

"May I help you?" Millstein says.

"This man is my husband," Oomieka says.

"I'd prefer you wait outside," the doctor responds. Oomieka identifies herself. He had not recognized her. He is a bit embarrassed, but still somewhat annoyed.

Nonetheless, he proceeds.

The pinch/snips are getting more painful.

171

"I'll do the one at the apex last," he says to the technician, for my benefit, but as if it were a decision she could countermand. "That will be the most painful because it is closest the nerve-endings near the opening of the anus."

I grit my teeth.

Pinnnnnnchrrrrr. "Try not to move," he says, after my body spasms. Rrrrrrip! I grunt-growl. "There, that wasn't so bad, was it?"

I want to ream his fucking asshole using a splintered fence post.

"You may lay there a while." As if I will ever want to walk again. He wipes my ass with some moistened swabs, washes his hands, then turns to the ultra-sound images.

I push myself to a sitting position, trying to ignore the lobster claws clenched about my testicles.

He points out the "stones" and "dark areas," mostly for Oomieka's benefit. They are offered to justify this de-sexing procedure. He then goes on to explain that I will have some vestiges of blood in my urine and my stool; that is if I can ever bring myself to piss or shit again. He says the blood in my semen will be more in evidence because the prostate is, after all, part of that system and it will take longer to disappear -- "two, maybe three weeks" -- because that system does not flush as frequently as the other two. Now, I certainly won't be wont to flush it as much as I have been. "It'll be rusty for a while. Not to alarm yourself." As Oomieka and I exit into the dry, snapping air, she brushes my cheek with her lips and asks if I feel up to driving. I nod, then waddle off to my Z.

48

I am pumping blood out the tip of my penis: rich, maroon strings of it. I have had spotting in my urine, stains of light brown on the white lining at the front of my briefs. There is no obvious blood in my stool. But this -- is not semen, "rust-colored" or otherwise. It is blood. I am bleeding internally. My system is *not* flushing, it is gushing. It seems fitting.

Oomieka says I am not hemorrhaging: "There'd be swelling, pain." Nonetheless, she suggests I notify the doctor. I call Millstein, get instead his nurse. She says I was told to go home and remain inactive. I tell her the doctor said no such thing. She reminds me the doctor informed me of this after-effect. I decide this is useless. Doctors are born to lie. I hang up. I decide upon a masturbatory frenzy, my idea of a flush.

I slip off into the family room, draw all the blinds, then pop in a porno tape I have secreted behind an abridged, two-volume set of the Oxford English Dictionary. I sit on the floor, with my back against a love seat, my pants at my ankles. I watch drawn-out sessions of finger-fucking, cunt-lapping, cock-sucking, multi-positional fucking with multiple partners, and finally a chocking load of cum, fired all over the rigid face of a less-than-fully-engaged, dish-water blonde (ersatz, I am guessing, but can't be sure because her cunt has been shaved slick). I am only medially excited, my level of excitement rising and ebbing in inverse proportion to my anticipation concerning the composition of the ejaculate.

Finally, a creamy load deposited at the rim of a gaping anus pushes me over the edge and my anus aches in sympathy to the rich, red striations I swipe across the Kleenexes I've draped between my spread legs. One shot clears the safety net and is sopped up by the rug. I feel the need to clean up after myself, but am immobilized.

I am going insane with this bleeding, this pumping blood instead of semen. I feel like the blood is pooling inside me, bloating my testicles like a water balloon or a wine skin. I want to puncture my flesh down there, drive a lance into my groin, let the blood flow out until the fluid turns milky again. I want . . . to . . . menstruate.

49

What next I bring thee shall please thee . . . thy
wish, exactly to thy heart's desire. Heart? What the fuck
was that?

All he wanted was someone to toss a football
around with him --

Yeah, tell me about it.

But, instead, he activated the little head and waited.

While they shouted out loud, the face in the crowd
was more than I anticipated.

Elohi, Elohi, lama shebaqtani.

What is it with this sexual drive? A yearning to
die? An insistence upon life -- at max participation?

The face in the crowd. Shit. She was pure. *He* got
in between. He was a shield. He turned the event. In an
instant. It was turned. She was pure. But I did not receive
the purity. What I got had been turned. It had been commandeered. He took the event. He fuckin' commandeered
it. The connection. He commandeered the fucking connection. God, I *loved* her. Do you hear that? I loved her. But
I misunderstood because *he* got in between. And it killed
me. And she died for it.

I am walking beneath an oak tree. It is a beautiful
tree: solid shaft of a trunk, beautiful crown. I've always
wanted an oak. I've owned a score of houses, with dozens
of trees, but never an oak. An oak and a lilac. I've always
wanted a lilac. I buy lilacs, plant them, but they develop
mold and die or, if they live, they never bloom. Now this
house, the one I live in now, it does not have an oak and
the lilac, an old established one, is shaded by a chestnut

tree and because it does not get direct sun, it does not bloom.

I am walking toward Aaley's apartment. I've never gone there without her leading or in tandem, or without an arrangement to see her. I am adrift, as I was in class, as I have been since the session with the young girl. From a distance, I can see someone sitting on the stone steps in front of the house where she lives. It is Aaley, I would know that if she were no bigger than a pencil prick. As I approach I can see that she is really not here but adrift herself. Adrift somewhere. Her thoughts, perhaps.

A little girl on a tricycle is riding on the opposite sidewalk. An older boy on a small bicycle is circling around her, showing off, asserting his dominance. He is a bit unsteady and has slowed the bike enough to force him to put his foot down. It is just enough of a delay to allow the little girl to catch him if he cannot get restarted quickly. She is peddling toward him, as fast as her little legs will allow. He pushes the bike back up and heads for his only escape, between two parked cars. A pick-up truck, having just turned onto the street, accelerates to twice the speed limit. I am almost to Aaley, but now she has become aware of the drama unfolding across the street. She fixes her gaze on the shadow beneath one of the parked cars. Suddenly a cat darts from the shadow and across the boy's path. He slams on his brakes and falls against one of the cars. The truck speeds by. The boy begins to cry. But then again, he did not die. Aaley turns to me. "I am *not* the embodiment of evil," she says, "because I have loved much."

She is searching my face for an answer, but I do not have one. At least I do not have the proper one.

"Come up stairs with me," she says.

"Are you sure?"

176

"It's why you've come, isn't it?"

"I'm not sure why I've come. I'm not sure of anything any more."

"You never were, Max, not this time."

She rises to her feet. "Come up with me, Max. Come rest. Rest your eyes. Rest your mind."

I am in the familiar confines of her bed. This is becoming the locus of my world. This is becoming my world. I am enveloped again in the warm orange glow from the small end-table lamp. My clothes are piled again in the arm chair opposite the footboard. This time I am frightened.

She is lying beside me, silent.

Her distance has played a major role in my disorientation. It is this mental, perhaps spiritual, distance that has distressed me. When she disappears for days, it is less of an absence than this. This absence in her presence is . . . disorienting. She disapproves of something. I think she disapproves of me. Period. But I don't understand. She has been a player. All along. Throughout. Things worked then. You can never count on things working over an extended period of time. Aaley *was* my connection. Was. I want a return. I want that back. I need some reinforcement.

"The blood does not bother me," she says, "I deal with it every month."

"With you, it is part of the natural order of things," I answer.

"Order? In nature?"

I don't answer. I don't want to veer off on a tangent.

"It is part of the recovery process for you," she says.

"I don't know."

177

She is on her back, studying the ceiling that has been a major source of interest for me during the past several months.

"I want to do it," I say.

"Do what?"

I let out an exasperated sigh.

"I'm not trying to be obtuse, Max. I want to know. What is it that we do?"

I want to say it is "fuck" that we do. I want to say it, but I don't. I don't want to say it. "I want to make . . . love," I say, instead.

"Do you, Max? Do you?"

"I don't know, Aaley. I don't know. Are we in love? Is that it? I don't know. For now, I mean for here and now, why don't we just content ourselves with . . . it."

She does not answer. She does not say no. She does not deny me.

I mount her in the missionary position. The physical union is soft and gentle. There is an exchange between my flesh and hers anywhere they come together. She kisses my mouth with lips moist and warm. Here, too, there is a sense of exchange. Something is different. It would seem that something is better, but I don't know. Now she is sharing something with me, giving something to me, but it is something that is already mine. She is giving something back, but what she is returning . . . is already mine. There is a sense that something in the past has become something in the present. There is the sense that something from the past has awakened something in the present. At the same time, I am feeling something go out of me and into her. But what has left me, has left no empty space. Where it was now feels fuller, more complete. As I approach orgasm, however, there is a shift.

Because I do not hope to turn again.[1]

But I do hope to turn. I shoot inside her. This is
my blood. There *is* a sense of emptiness. There is a void.
Because I *do* hope to turn. I want a return. There is a
sense that I must move to some place better, now. But I do
not want to go there. Something is tugging at me. Something will not let go. I want to stay. I choose to stay. I insist upon staying.

Aaley is crying, silently. Her face is wet with tears.
She takes a handful of her long, black hair and wipes at the
tears on her cheeks, but they are replaced with new tears.
She is warm and her skin is emitting her smell. It is the familiar smell, the one she emits whenever we have sex, but
it is more than that. It is a memory for me. But I cannot
place it. It is a fond memory. It is a sad memory. But I
cannot place it.

Aaley pushes me off, then slides down my body.

She begins caressing me feet. Her hands are velvet.
She runs them over and over my feet. My feet are dried
and cracked, parched and flaking, but her hands are soft
and have grown moist. They transfer this moisture to my
feet. They soften them, as if rubbing them in fine oil. It is
as if she emits a kind of natural ointment. She is kneading
my toes, lightly stroking the instep, the arch, the ball and
the heel. It is at once erotic and incredibly soothing. I approach a swoon . . .

But it is troubling to me, this supplicant's posture.
Rise, Aaley, rise.

And why does she feel compelled to assume it?
Perhaps in supplication to a position I'd arrogated to my-
self. Perhaps a position I would seek to retrieve, to retain.
No.

Rise, Aaley, rise. And shine.

179

Her eyes search mine.
Probe behind.
With trepidation seek the scream and smother it.
For now.
Her eyes join mine.
And find, the glow, the shine, lost in time.
Unquantified.
"I love you, Max, I'm fine."
"I know, so'm I'm."
The jism, this time, is rust-colored. My concern abates.

Why have I ravaged her? Why has she let me? Assisted me? When I push my finger against the sphincter, she cries out. I recoil. Finally, limits. No more a hotbed of perversity.[2] She is moaning. I cannot imagine why. I can't imagine I have disgusted her so.

"Cut your fingernails before you come here next time," she declares.

I am perplexed.

"One woman's perversity is another's passion," she says.

50

It hasn't helped. The session with Aaley has left a great hole. A great, round, black hole. It is a hole of my own creating. I am being sucked into it. I am trying to hold onto the edges, but I am on the inside of a balloon and someone has untied the neck. The air is rushing out and it is taking me with it as it flies about the universe, unchecked. I want to tie a board across my ass to stop me from being sucked out, down the hole. The big hole. The great, round, black hole. But I cannot stop the rush. I am sucked through and into the great force of the suction. It is sucking the air out of me. I cannot breathe. I cannot breathe. Something is stopping the air to my lungs. I cannot breath. "Help!" my mind cries, but my mouth says nothing. "Help!" I do not want to die, but I do not want to cause a scene, either, by crying for help. "Help . . . ?"

I am awake. My legs are over the side of the bed. Oomieka has her arms around my abdomen, her hands joined with the fingers wrapped tightly in a double-fist under my rib cage. I cannot breathe. No air will pass through my windpipe. She pulls in and up with a blow that must have taken all her delicate strength. I expectorate a great glob of phlegm. Air rushes into my lungs. I take a half-dozen great gulps of it, then "shit!" I shout.

"It's not time for you to die, Max," she replies, then gets up and goes into the bathroom to pee. When she returns to bed, she says, "get some sleep, Max."

"What happened?"

"You've got to do something about that post-nasal drip."

181

"I'm sorry," I reply, "I'll try not to die any more tonight."

"Go back to sleep. I've got surgery first thing in the morning."

Right.

51

"Norton is burnt up, says I can't see you any more."

"What?"

"It's too stressful."

"What is?"

"Our relationship."

"What relationship?" *Norton knows about the hand-job.*

"I can't sleep nights. It re-ignites the conflict in my being."

My being.

"What does?"

"Our relationship."

Again? "The blindness thing?"

"No.

"The man/woman."

Norton cares?

"Norton says it is affecting . . . my touch."

Too much. His effective reattachment of my brain has taken the magic from her touch, drained it away, so to speak.

"He is very resentful."

So what.

"I'm afraid he may come looking for you."

Boing!

"And if I stop seeing you?"

"That will help, but only if I can get back my touch."

Is this a plea? And, if so, to whom? What can I do?

"I'll do what I can," I answer with no intention to do anything except depart this lover's . . . quadrilateral? I

183

turn to go. He stops me with hand upon my shoulder, a heavy hand.

"My God, Max, you weren't just . . . workin' it out, were you?"

I keep my silence.

"My God."

He releases his grip. "Max," she says, "you knew what would happen when you brought this to me."

"Yes. You were the only one who could direct me."

"Yes, thanks to me you are the savior of Thebes.[1] And look what it has gotten me: the loss of my identity."

"I see."

"Not like me."

Only If you never come to know yourself.

But I come to know myself, albeit someone somewhat different from whom I had imagined. Shit, it is happening now, as we speak. It is not a prediction; it is a premonition; not optative subjunctive, but the object of the preposition, assumed though unexpressed; deconstructed, of course. Time compressed to zero in the mind of a blind man who cannot see reality, only what is. His curse. She sugar-coated it; she was being kind to me.

"O.K., I'll leave."

She sighs as if she knows it will not be enough. "You'll leave me as you found me?"

"I cannot say for sure."

He looks at me askance, a touch of anger creeps across his weighted cheeks.

"Probably not. You had it: the energy exchange. It can be intense when you elect to fuck with fate."

"I gave you a massage, Max, nothing more."

Kill the messenger. "We both know better."

I exit without resolution.

184

52

Dr. Vera Victoria took over the OB/GYN Department at the hospital where Oomieka works about two years ago. She lobbied for the position, cooed, cajoled and coddled the search committee, then the board of trustees, maybe even sucked a cock or two. The hospital agreed to a three-year contract, negotiated by her husband, a legal snake in the rock music business. The Vickster, as she is known to the staff of underlings, all of whom she treats like shit, is a stick-figured, tight-assed cunt, who wears her sewage-colored hair back in a roll so taut it looks like her eyes are trying to catch up with her ears in opposing orbits around her head. If you study her, dispassionately for a moment or two, you sense a modicum of physical appeal -- perhaps it is in the sheer severity of her appearance -- but her demeanor shouts bitch so loudly any sense of attraction is drowned out. I, of whom it is said would fuck anyone, would walk away. Fantasizing her in the vilest of couplings does not elicit so much as a twinge in my scrotum. Oomieka, who hates no one, hates the Vickster. Oomieka, whose mortal enemy is death, wishes the Vickster dead.

I have concluded that Dr. Victoria is evil, innately so. It is why she torments my wife. For every moment she diverts Oomieka from her medical rounds, someone suffers the loss, loses some segment of time off her allotment on the planet. In effect, The Vickster disrupts destiny . . . fulfills destiny.

"You have to bring her down," I say over a quickly concocted late dinner of pasta and canned clam sauce.

"Don't be ridiculous. She is the department chairperson; I am just a . . . "

185

"What? Just a . . . doctor?"

"Yes."

"Precisely."

Oomieka has related to me how the Vickster has called a meeting of senior administrators for the unexpressed purpose of attacking my wife's reputation. "She thinks I have been dishonest about my secretary's salary," Oomieka says, "charging it at one hundred percent to two separate grants." It is simply procedure until one or both is/are approved, then the salary is allocated proportionately according to the predicted workload for each. "It would have taken a two-minute phone call to explain this. What does she think I intend to do with the second salary, shift it to a Swiss account?"

"That's not the point. She knocks two hours out of your day and she reduces your medical effectiveness while you prepare to respond -- or even when you're simply worrying over it."

"But why would she keep me from my patients?"

The Vickster is trying to win the unwinnable, divert the ultimate, overall destiny, forestall the moment when she assumes her final position in the eternal blackness, and recruit as many as she can to keep her company. She is death. She is bad death.

"Fear."

"Fear? Don't be ridiculous."

"She is afraid of you. You are what she is not. You are a doctor."

Her face relaxes, for a moment, almost to a smile, but then tenses again. I hate this. Despite our differences over the fulfillment of my perverted fantasies, I know who my wife is: Dr. Yes to the Vickster's Dr. No.

186

"You have to take her on. If you don't she will kill your patients and she will do it through you. You will be her accomplice."

Hurt sweeps across Oomieka's face. I am sorry I have said what I have said, but she has been uncharacteristically tunnel-visioned here. She has fought death as a concept, never as a reality. She has battled its symptoms, never its substance. It will take everything she has to fight this battle because the Vickster will force Oomieka to sacrifice some of those in her charge to fight the battles along the way. But the loss will be far greater if she does not.

"I've got a splitting headache," she says. "I will take a pill and go to bed."

I want to hold her, but it does not happen. I am deeply saddened. I want to cradle her head upon my shoulder, but the opportunity does not present itself. I want a different ending, but I cannot affect the alteration. I am impotent. Ignorant. Gone.

53

I have walked the road along the beach all the way into the village. It is a day that should be warmer than it is, the temperature moderated by a soft, though inconsistent, breeze off the bay and a relatively high humidity. Finches tweet from the cover of thick hemlock hedges and flit between there and the branches of maples, large oaks and copper beeches that are common near my home. Where the commercial area begins, the sidewalkless street that runs through the residential area erupts suddenly into a concrete slab as if two giant geological plates have come edge to edge under the village and one of them has been forced to the surface. This sidewalk rims the rows of small stores which comprise the village: first the hardware store with new red-bedded wheel barrows standing upright against one wall; the army/navy store bedecked in a window display that has not changed markedly since the end of World War Two; boutiques that replace owners on a weekly basis; and The FOG, which I whizz past without daring a sideways glance.

The sidewalk descends to the harbor just before Bernie's, a big seafood restaurant built out onto a quay which defines the northern boundary of the marina. Wharfs, finger piers and moorings confine sailboats and oversized, overpowered power boats bobbing in their berths. There is a boatyard at the southern rim of the marina; masts of sailboats in drydock, their undersides stripped and shamelessly bare, engine blocks cradled aloft in chain metal slings.

It is early lunchtime and one of the marine mechanics is seated against an iron piling eating a sandwich and reading Pound's "Cantos." His bottle of Coke is balanced delicately on a sawed-off wood piling adjacent. It's an eclectic part of the world, what can I say?

I stop for a moment and feign a contemplative look out at the water, but I am really watching the man read and eat. His brows are alternately knitted and relaxed, confusion followed by comprehension returning to confusion. I wonder how he is handling the oriental pictographs. On the other hand, he *is* facing toward the east, where the sun is still just shy of its high point. The words of one of the Cantos sings across my mind. But I cannot remember more than the one, free- ranging couplet. I apply my own conclusion. Then move on.

I cut through an alley alongside Bernie's, then take a weathered-wood staircase down to the shore. The beach is pebbly here, geologic crumbs left by the last glacier. The pebbles are a deep, unnatural hepatic orange, groupings of which are swathed in wraps of seaweed gone black through exposure to the air. The water is still icy cold and it is very clear. It is a lifeless clarity, however, a clarity that somehow does not convey a sense of well-being. I want to know it still contains bacteria, protozoa, small plants, plankton, but the water is as dead as a pane of glass. Around the large boulders strewn beneath the wharf pilings are white layers of salt, near-perfect rings at some kind of supernaturally determined level. The salt crystals do not sparkle, but are blunted by the effects of the elements, the very elements that created them. They ring the rocks like termite tunnels erupted along the skin of a tropical tree. Gulls parade along the beach, waddling from side to side, mimicking windup toys on the sidewalk in the city. They are scavenging fish carcasses dropped from the restaurant above. The food in that place has not been the same since old man Bernie died. I toss a pebble in the gulls' direction, but they ignore it. Perhaps they have become too bloated to fly. There is a puddle just beyond a hillock, ten yards from the slope of the wet, hard-packed sand. It is refilled by each incoming tide, left by each ebb, then drained by the sun. It is, each time, the death trap for an indeterminate number of killies. Each time the circle recedes into itself, they race about in a frantic search to find the escape from the shrinking circle. But, of course, there is none.

The sun is the size of a pie plate, a perfect disk in the hazy sky. Haze seems to be the default position of the sky around me these days. I don't remember much of the blue there once was. There is a dot beneath the disk that I take to be an illusionary spot lingering in my eye, caused by staring at the blunted sun. With my hand, I shield the sun. The spot remains.

A point. With no explanation.

The killies swim frantically until the circle disappears.

Equilibrium.

It is making me dizzy.

Equilibrium.

The point at the origin of the Big Bang?

I see it.

It is there.

The position of arrested animation.

Peace.

The still point at the center of the turning universe.

All else is chaotic. Something is clarifying for me, like the clarity of the water in the bay. Where I seek order there is none. It is a deception. The expansion of the universe is degradation into disorder. The formulas tell us that; the second law of thermodynamics. All will disorder while the acceleration slows to zero. Then the universe collapses into itself . . . contracts to the point.

190

The point.

The transition to heaven?

Motion is reality. Lack of motion is spirituality. That is the point.

At the freeze frame, there is total knowledge, all the combined elements of the natural world compressed into a dimensionless point. All smells, fragrant and foul; all substance, polished and pitted; colors compressed to white; molecules de-combinant to their basic selves . . . the flower deflowered. Perfection.

My cock and Aaley's cunt together forever, at last. My cock and the cunt of Sue Graf from class together at last. My mind and Oomieka's -- one. My mind and Einstein's -- one. My mind and . . . Hitler's -- one. Mine and Pound's. Mine and Simeon's. Shit! Knowledge is not the expansion of the mind. Knowledge returns with the *contraction* of the universe. We did know most at the moment of birth, then add confusing information until we die. But is our original birth the "Big Bang"?

Of course.

Time after that is a kind of messy regeneration of what's already here. As we hurtle further from the point, the search becomes more involved, the answers more complicated. Everything is hurtling too far apart; once we had it all in one place. Expansion is a kaleidoscope with ever-more-complicating forms. But real knowledge is in simplicity, not complexity. Complexity is a card-trick for smart people. Book smart. Stock market smart. Retail store smart. Bullshit-religion smart. A single formula explains

. . . all.

Cogito ergo sum?

Not sure.

I think not.

191

Only when knowledge is compressed to the unity, does it become pure. It becomes faith, it becomes . . . the love of God. I am recycled matter, recycled thoughts; the older I get, the less I understand. I am an ignorant creature, corrupted by sin and clinging to life because I fear pain and death. The universe is a continuing mutation of truth. Existence is part of the process, but irrelevant to the final conclusion. I am a fifty-one-year-old man reading John Milton, Boethius, Thomas Browne, Emerson, Thoreau, Dickinson, Whitman, Pound, Eliot. I am worried about the way I look, because I want to get pussy . . . for no relevant reason, because we will all be compressed back into the point. Everything that has ever existed will be compressed into that point and we will experience it all

    . . . at once.

We will understand it all

    . . . at once.

We will be it. Everything will be us. We will be everything -- at the point. We *are* everything at the point -- now. There is no future. There is no past. There is only now. The point at the origin of the Big Bang is a metaphysical answer to a scientific question, arrived at by scientists. It is the point where reality *joins* revelation. And the point

    . . . is

    . . . but a single thought in the mind of God.

Zero.

I am dizzy, fall against one of the pilings. It is slimed in green moss. It smells of decay. Life sprouting from decay. I am breathing rapidly. Hyperventilating. I drop to my knees, try to get the blood back into my head, demand my heart do its job and fight the effects of gravity. The gulls waddle off. Give me a wide circle.

I regain my composure. Walk to the staircase, grip the rotted handrail, pray I make it back.

At night I write, "A block of air to sculpt.[1]"

At the far end of the splintered planking
in the marina where the glitter boats oscillate
to the echoes of the waves,
a troubadour, returned from the dead,
sits beside a rusted piling
and sings new songs according to the old method.

"Sweet cries and cracks
                    and lays and chants inflected,
turn tears and rack
                    from serum now infected."

His face
is shaken loose.
His mind
is in full flight.

Miglior Fabbro[2] is nervous, but undaunted.
He has passed this way before.
He has passed on the ham and cheese with a classic
        Coke
to glide along the quay, maintaining a low profile.
He is late of the asylum.
I walk beside him
much less certain than he that there will be enough
        volume
to serve our purposes
. . . that there will be anything at all.

The water has gone crystal clear, oil of vitriol.
The detritus is long gone.
The wavelets leave rings around the rocks

along the shore.
Matter;
No matter.
But our search does not involve water.
He looks up. I
watch the course for slippery rocks.

"I've spent a life-time window-shopping for body-
          dressing.
(He is unmoved by driveling.)
I need a block of air to sculpt."

Night has fallen like a dumptruck
and the singer glows in the dark.
He's been joined by razorheads
and suits blowing noseflutes.

Fabbro lifts a transparent finger to the eastern sky.
At first, I don't see it.
Then I do:
the morning star.

"It was not in that spot yesterday," I observe.
"The point exactly."
He smiles and disappears into an unfinished poem.
I take up my pen
and wonder.

54

Oomieka's dispassionate analysis of the meeting is to call it a draw.

"I gave as good as I got," she says.

She is disappointed that some of the executives were not more supportive in view of her two decades of service at the hospital, her impeccable reputation for honesty and integrity, her many community service appearances and her representation of the hospital as a spokesperson in print and broadcast media.

"They are afraid for their jobs," she alibis. "She was trying to bully me. It was my turn. They let it play out."

"They're not even part of her chain of command."

"She has a great deal of influence."

"They are cowards."

Oomieka is dog tired, drawn, mentally drained. It frightens me to see her this way. She is always lively, ready -- anxious -- to engage, bright, often brilliant with her answers. It frightens me to see her look the way I often feel. It is the diversion from her mission, the misappropriation of her time.

"What are you going to do?"

"Engage her. You were right. It is my only option."

I was right?

Why now?

Why this time?

There is no time.

"I'm sorry. You don't deserve this."

"I'll deal with it. That's life."

No. It is the usurpation of life.

"I'm here for you." *I am. I think. I . . . wish?*
"Thank you."
I can't read her expression.
"No, really. Thank you."

55

Simeon's secretary has called to say the chairman would like to see me. Lately, our sessions have only been critiques of some aspect of my professional or personal behavior. It has become tiresome. I decide to try to redirect whatever the fuck is on his mind, at least partially. Earlier in the day, I send him the poem for his feedback. I know he will recognize the references to Pound. I am hoping it will impress him.

"I am suspending you, Max," he says, before I can ask him what he thought. "I will take your class through the end of the semester. That's a pain in the ass for me, I've got to tell you, but I gotta do what I gotta do."

"I don't get it," I muster. "I thought I was conducting things the way you wanted them."

"Until your last class."

"What about it?"

"You walked in, babbled pieces of just about everything Milton had written -- all of it in less than fifteen minutes -- then dismissed the class."

"I had something on my mind."

"We all have things *on our minds*, Max. But we all have responsibilities to the students, the university --"

"I have a greater responsibility to myself."

"Yourself?"

"Who is it we are talking about here?"

"She's fucked you up, Max. I warned you about her. But she has some sort of hold on you. It's really amazing to think that you of all people would be susceptible to this sort of thing. That you would not keep it in perspective."

197

"I won't get you angry by questioning what it is you're talking about. But I have to tell you I don't know what you're talking about."

"She's just a pussy, Max. Read your own poetry. Pay attention to your own advice."

"I would have preferred anger to blatant sexism."

His eyes turn to fire. "It's got nothing to do with my particular prejudices. It has to do with the delusions you have concocted concerning this relationship. I've told you what she's done elsewhere. What she is doing to you is what she does. She is a whore, Max."

I shake my head. "That girl is extraordinary. She has been a great inspiration to me."

"Oh pa-lease."

"She has been the inspiration for much of what I've written in the last several months."

"She has been the inspiration for the chin-deep river of shit you find yourself drowning in."

I shake my head, again. "You can't handle this, can you, Simeon? I've got something going here that is bothering the shit out of you and my 'problems' so to speak have nothing to do with me. It's a matter of what other people can or cannot handle."

He sighs. "I told them I'd handle this, Max. But I'm not playing with you any more. The only reason you're not out on your ass totally and completely is I talked him into the suspension. I want you to see it as your last chance."

"I do see my last chance. Very clearly."

"Max, I don't want to do this to you. You must help me."

"I don't know what to tell you, Simeon. I don't *know* what's going to happen."

198

He shakes his head. He reaches down, opens the file drawer in his desk and removes a couple of sheets of paper.

He places them on his desk. "This poem," he begins, "it scares the shit out of me."

"We're getting a bit melodramatic, now, aren't we?"

"Fabbro went nuts, Max. He made broadcasts for the fascists and ended up in a lunatic asylum -- which was the only way the American authorities could justify not executing the son-of-a-bitch."

"That's all bullshit and you know it, Simeon. It was the party line. He was a brilliant writer who was speaking his mind and they didn't know how to shut him up. That 'lunatic asylum' became the center of the civilized world until he died."

"Is that what you're doing then? Is Pound your role model? Are you determined to follow him into some sort of self- imposed exile?"

"He is a role model to the extent that he demanded perfection."

"This obsession with writing the perfect poem, again? No one gives a shit. Write what you must, Max, but understand, no one gives a shit."

"Tell me, Simeon, look me in the eye and tell me *you* don't give a shit. Tell me none of the writing you've read during all these years when we were masquerading as literature professors had an impact. Tell me you don't have one ounce of respect for those who insisted upon perfection, who were willing to starve before they gave up on it. Tell me you don't feel some sense of admiration, that when something you read clicks you don't want to cry out 'thanks, you crazy son-of-a-bitch, thanks!' Tell me you don't give a shit, Simeon."

He looks at me. For an instant there is a spark of true respect, but it falls to earth and winks out in something that looks -- again, for just an instant -- like jealousy.

"It's not the point," he says. "Do what you want, do whatever the fuck it is you need to do in the confines of your room, Max, but teach the fuckin' classes the way the syllabus dictates. In essence, I'm giving you the rest of the semester off. Take some time to think this through, Max. Come back to me in one piece."

A smile glints in my brain. Aaley. We will have more time together. *We* will work this -- what ever *this* is -- we will work this through.

He is looking at me askance. "You're just going to go on fucking with that coed, aren't you?"

"I'll see you next semester."

56

I guess this thing with the suspension is not unexpected; perhaps it has even been what I've been pressing for all along. In any event, I don't give a damn about it, one way or the other. Oomieka will be upset, but not because of any potential loss in pay. She will be upset because she has viewed the demands of my class as having a moderating effect on my bouts with creative madness. This will scare the hell out of her. I can't make up my mind whether to tell her or not.

I wander over to the campus coffee shop, as is my custom on the days of my classes, for a cup of coffee and one of those small, cellophane-wrapped, over-priced, circles of coffee crumb cake. In a booth in a corner by one of the windows are five of my Milton students: Unlaced Sneakers, B-S B and Sue Graf, along with two who do little more than take up space.

My entrance has caused them discomfort. The buzzing has buzzed out. They stiffen in their seats, their face muscles tighten. It's too good to pass up. I walk over.

I stand before their table but do not speak. The tension is more pronounced then it has been in some of my recent classes. I let the silence hang.

Finally, one of the space-takers says, "would you like to sit down, professor?"

There is an empty seat at their table, but I decide to take one at the unoccupied table adjacent. I can engage in whatever exchange is about to take place from there and I can exit without obstruction whenever I decide to.

"I'll not be conducting the class any more this semester," I offer, "but I guess you know that already."

201

No one speaks for a second or two, then Sue Graf replies, "yes." She diverts her eyes back to her cup of tea.

"I guess I've had trouble getting through to you."

Again, no answer. Finally, Unlaced Sneakers has had enough of his camouflaged campaign to remove me. He decides it's time to step out of the shadows. "You haven't taught us anything," he says.

It is an unfocused remark, a typically weak attack. I decide to toy with him.

"I'm sure you've learned something?"

"No," he says, "nothing."

He is pathetic. I smile. "And the rest of you, the same is true for all of you?"

Nothing. They are very unsettled by my presence. I guess that just prior to my appearance, US had been pontificating about how I got what I deserved and they had been letting him rant, but not necessarily agreeing, at least not fully. On the other hand, they don't want to take on either he or me.

"Look," I say, "It's not a matter of what I teach. It's a matter of whether you begin to understand."

Eyebrows furrow.

"Understand what?" Unlaced Sneakers says. He is obviously the only one who is going to engage me. And, now that he has shed his cover, he is warming to the full-frontal assault.

I shake my head.

"You're the worst teacher I've ever had," he says.

I spit out a laugh.

"No, really," he says, motioning with his hand to take in the rest of the group. "You are the worst teacher we've ever had."

202

"Come on, Jason," Sue Graf cuts in. But the tremble in her voice betrays her less-than-total commitment to my defense.

"No," US persists, "he's the worst fucking teacher I've ever had." It's pathetic, really, how he has become further emboldened by my loss of any control over him, as if this somehow manages to reclaim some of the ground he has lost all semester by exposing himself as an asshole -- with my assistance, of course. "You are," he repeats, to continue his stoning. "You are the worst teacher I've ever had."

Had.

Past.

History.

Freedom.

I don't give a shit about him. About my job with the university. About teaching. There is a sudden rush. A complete sense of freedom. Accomplishment. At having finally arrived at some place. Cloture.

"Why thank you," I reply, with a smile. "Then I *have* gotten through to you."

Hatred wells up from the guts of Unlaced Sneakers. He begins to rise out of his chair. Absurdly, he has decided to take me on -- physically. But his power is no match for mine. It's odd but I feel no hatred toward him; he somehow does not seem to warrant it. He is not even a worthy adversary. I stare him back into place simply by conveying to him that he is no match for me.

Refrain thy tongue blasphémous. Eternal wrath burn'd after him to the bottomless pit.[1]

"Don't tempt me," I say and stand.

I turn and head for the door, not concerned in the least about the eyes that follow my retreat.

203

57

My curtain call at the lounge. Andy is carping.
Bart is on a short leash. Imbalance. Askew. Off kilter. Angelica is encubed. Even Simeon is alone in his own space.
And I . . . am smokin'. I am dealin' with the power thing.
Gettin' a grip on the gist of the grist of the upcoming conference. Yes. I have been drinkin'. It's a sin wherein I am
unprepared, unaware of the requirements of the world per
se. It was a liquid lunch. Sorry. I feel stupid, Cupid, unwise. Surprise!

Power?

Unwise.

A connection. A missed connection. A unholy connection. If you haven't a clue, kick ass to cover your short-
coming. Short coming? No' me, mahn.

"Maax?"

"Huh?"

"It's annoying."

"Whah? Angelica, wha . . . t?"

"That gibberish you're babbling."

You can hear me? "Sorry, just thinking out loud.

"Thinking?"

It's snide. I don't like snotty when I've been drinking. I am prone to mood shifts. Snide will shift me.

"Forgive me. I didn't realize the machinations of
my mind were conducted at some lower circle in the universe of thought." My peeve cannot overcome my dysfunc-
tional tongue and lips. I have fumbled the Ls, Ms and
THs. My sluggish reflexes have even held my facial pose
a moment too long. Now I feel I appear pathetic. I smile,
stupidly.

She smiles . . .
Cunt.

58

They are preparing to terminate Oomieka's contract. She doesn't see it, but I do; the cowards control the company and they will follow the path of least resistance. Oomieka feels her record, her years of seniority, her large patient population, etc., will hold sway; the cowards will leave her unprotected, in the flames, but they will not let her go. If for no other reason than the revenues she represents.

"In most situations, I'd agree with you," I offer. "Money talks, bullshit walks. But, this is a power struggle. The Vickster is executing members of the opposition party. She will rebuild from the ruins. She feels *her* reputation and the new doctors she selects will hold the patients."

"How the hell do you know all this?" Oomieka snaps. "You're not there on a daily basis. You don't experience the interplay."

"It's why I can provide a dispassionate assessment. I've seen her type. I've seen them operate. Shit, Oomieka, I'm an academician."

Again, I have depressed her. Again, I am right; her eyes say so.

"We'll see," is her weak reply.

This is scaring the hell out of me.

59

Amanda hates me. She feels her mother made a terrible mistake marrying me. This is, of course, an obvious incongruity. She is very bright.

Amanda hates life. I have a better chance with Sarah.

60

Which is why I chose Amanda.

I have been standing at the threshold of her room for pregnant moments without acknowledgment. She is wearing the headphones from her stereo and began a pronounced headbob shortly after I darkened her doorway. Now it is a contest of wills. I will lose. I must make the more aggressive move. I am at a complete loss. Step back; retreat. Step forward; attack; swat her upside the head. Of course, neither.

I step into the room, sit on the bed alongside. She stares straight ahead at the wall. I consider switching off the stereo, pulling the plug, throwing the stereo through the window.

"Amanda," I say, "may I have a word with you?"

She smirks, removes the headphones, lays them on her desk, turns to confront me.

"Is it important?" she counters in pure disgust. The headphones leak tinny music across the surface of the desk.

"Yes, I'd say it is."

"Then what?"

"How are you doing?"

She tsks. "Fine, and you?" she says, matter-of-factly.

I sigh. "I don't want to fight."

"Good," she says and reaches for the headphones.

"Amanda!"

"What?!"

"Why are we fighting?"

"Who wants to know?"

"Me . . . your father?"

"Is that a question?"

I shake my head, push myself across the bed and lean my back against the wall. "I'm not leaving."

"As you wish," she says and reaches for the head-phones.

I make no move to stop her.

She fits them in place and turns up the music. She reaches for a magazine, then begins leafing through the pages.

I sit, watch her. She is stone. She is . . . who? Her mother? Me? What we've made of her? None of the above. I shift back to the floor, rise, leave the room.

Amanda needs to hate me. I am fucking with that.

61

It is enough to make a body ashamed of the human race.

The Vickster is hamboning the powers that be and they are buying it because they got no balls, and Oomieka is bleeding some more. I am dying watching this because it is disrupting the one rock-solid constant in my life. The clutch-straw that keeps my head from going under.

The Vickster is diverting patients away from Oomieka and referring new ones to any of a host of incompetent assholes she has installed in the already crowded offices and exam rooms. She has added excess staff to accelerate cash flow and divert attention from the degradation of services, which will ultimately wrap parentheses around the key figures on the bottom line.

Oomieka has met with the senior administrative official at the hospital to protest the Vickster's brass attempts to take over her grants. Dr. Victoria's programs for the department have been, in sum, a financial disaster and she wants to commandeer Oomieka's well-run, positive-cash-flow grants to cover some of her losses. Oomieka has been administering these programs for years. They are, in a very real sense, hers, not the hospital's.

"She is within her authority, as department chair," Dr. Abrams says.

"No previous department chair has ever seen fit to do this," Oomieka protests.

"That was their choice. She chooses otherwise."

"These grants earn money for the hospital," Oomieka replies. "Dr. Victoria will drain the funds --"

"According to our analyses, they lose money," Dr. Abrams cuts in.

"That's not true."

"Factor in physical plant, amortization of equipment, supplies --"

"I account for all that. We use a formula."

"Apparently, the formula is in error."

"According to whom?"

Dr. Abrams does not answer.

Oomieka stares at him, shakes her head.

"The hospital thinks it might be a good idea if you considered early retirement," Dr. Abrams says. He avoids eye contact.

"I'm years from retiring."

"It's a recommendation. A strong recommendation. There will be an attractive severance package . . ."

"I haven't dedicated my life to . . . an attractive package."

He smiles idiotically.

"She smiled at me in the hallway outside his office," Oomieka tells me. "If she'd had a hat on, she would have tipped it."

"What are you going to do?"

"I'm leaving, taking the grant programs with me. Two-point- three million in annual revenue. It'll push the department down the toilet."

"And that's what you want?"

"Nooo. That's not what I want, but what are my alternatives?"

I don't have any. And by the way, my gravy train is dropping over the side of the trestle.

"What about your co-workers, the nurses? What will happen to them with you gone?"

"What do you want me to say, Max?"

211

"Where will you go? How will you administer your grants, tend to your patients until you relocate?"

She stares at me with doleful eyes. She doesn't have the answers. I can't remember when she didn't have the answers. I would have thought she'd anticipate something like this. Sooner or later, it happens to everyone. But not Oomieka. To me, to others, to the Vickster, but not Oomieka. "Max," she says in a voice I don't recognize, "I have wished her dead."

"It's a common reaction, Oomieka."

The eyes are fixed, the steady doleful stare. Now I understand.

"It's a common reaction," I repeat.

Precisely.

God, the universe is in chaos. Oomieka is adrift. *Tachycardia.* So this *is* the way the world ends, not with a bang but a whimper?[1]

62

I am fearful, uncharacteristically. Generally I find the sounds and sights of the woods pleasant. This time, I am chilled. There is a crack deep in the woods, followed by a ground-shaking thud, then, off to my right, an odd ruse of leaves in a maple sapling -- nothing else moving on either side.

An immature sparrow is in the road before me, near the center of the lane, pecking periodically at the road grit. A car emerges at the turn from the beach and accelerates toward us. I step into the road and walk the direct line between the white Honda and the pale brown bird. We are converging on the point in a three-way game of chicken. The bird seems unconcerned. I am filled with fear, but unconcerned with the outcome here. I stare into the driver's eyes. The bird flies. I step aside. The driver gives me the finger. I am relieved.

At the Burgess Estate, the garbage cans are turned over, again. My thought is Bottom-Feeder has lost it, is scavenging for steak bones or something, but the tears through the white plastic of the trash bags is classic raccoon. He'd even managed to pull the lids aside, despite their being secured with bungee straps.

A cardinal is singing a chorale somewhere nearby. A red- winged blackbird glides from a weeping limb of a horse chestnut to a swaying waystation on a cattail in the marsh on the far side of a mown-grass knoll. In the midst of the knoll sits a metal cage. The raccoon stands helpless in the trap. He is a big one and he's been neutralized. I wonder if it's legal, in this state, to trap animals. I don't think it is. If it isn't what do the Burgesses intend to do

213

with their prisoner? And why do I give a shit? I decide I
don't and continue on toward the beach.

There is a definite chill in the air. It *is* a chilly day,
but it's not that kind of chill. I sense the presence of something threatening. No, the sensation still builds. It is not
here yet, but approaching. It is death, circling. I am alone,
a respite in one of my thinking-walks. There is no one to
turn to for help. That's the way it is: born alone; die alone.

Walter bursts upon me from behind a row of dead
hedges that separate the beach from the foot of Sound
Beach Road. His lumpish form hurtles at me through a
web of snapping sticks and the sweep of dried leaves. I am
leaning against the fractured granite chunks of the breakwater which defines the east end of the tiny town beach. I am
taking my second drag on a freshly lit cigarette, my feet un-
grounded in loose sand. He is upon me before I am sure
what's hit me, even before I determine who he is.

My feet slip in the loose earth. I go down on one
knee, slip around him to one side, am free, momentarily,
stand up. But I hesitate. The moment is lost. There is no
time to run. Then again, there is no place to hide. He is
my neighbor.

Thou shalt not covet thy neighbor's wife.

He grunts as he drives his shoulder into my mid-
section. With an expulsion of air, I am driven back against
the breakwater. The edge of a ragged granite boulder digs
into my backbone. "Wa-Walter?" I blurt out in a staged
stutter. "What the?"

He is trying to work his hands around my back, but
his arms are too short. I slip under them, again, take a step
back, then turn and face him. Again, I consider running,
but I still don't have an answer re where to go. It's pathetic, but denial appears my only option.

214

"What are you doing, Walter?" I blurt at him, an-
grily.

"You walked all over me, Max," he answers. His
face is as red as a party balloon. "I thought you were my
friend."

Walking on Walter? What is this guy talking
about? We've had no previous contact beyond my deflect-
ing a couple of the idiotic comments he'd let fall over the
fence a spring or summer ago, when, like this, he'd burst
upon me without warning, before I could duck away.

I put my thoughts into words. "What are you talking about?"

"You know what I'm talking about." You *know*.

"No, Walter, I don't *know*."

"Ruth. You know her?"

In the Biblical sense, you are asking, I presume?

"Your wife?"

His eyes combust.

I back off. At least I attempt to. "Lovely woman,"
is the best I can do. I almost laugh.

His anger escalates. His face reddens further. It is
halfway between rose and crimson.

"She told me," he grunts.

I dismiss "Told-you-what?" immediately.

Of course I had seen this coming, but chose to ignore its probability. This has been scripted by Bags, of
course. It is the revenge she has been not-so-subtlely allud-
ing to. She is playing her trump. Walter. She has known
all along that Walter would only do what he was forced to
do. Now, Walter has come at me with a passion never
aroused in his relationship with Bags. This is *not* about the
violation of the sanctity of his marriage to Ruth. He has
known about the affair all along. It was a convenience for
him, relieving the need to justify his unusually late union

215

meetings. (I always felt he'd chosen an unpredictably literary term for his little dodge -- inadvertently, of course.) But once Ruth goes public with us, even if the audience were confined to just Walter and me, his blue-collar mentality, with its fraudulent sense of honor, demands he do something about it. I'm sure he is sure he can even justify killing me, under the unwritten right to retribution of the husband cuckolded. Then, once acquitted, he is justified in the continuance of his menu of sins, with the added entrée of being free to brutalize a wife who is an admitted adulterer. Of course, Ruth, at that point, is long gone, shacked up seven states away with some tattooed biker, or a skinny-as-a-split-rail hop-head with a cock like a fire hose. And Walter is at a permanent union meeting with Rosie O'Grady.

We return now to our movie, wherein Walter is pushing me backwards . . . toward the water. He's doing that two-palms- against-the-chest pump-push which is the opening round of all street-corner brawls. And his arms are like a couple of horizontal pile-drivers. He's a strong little brute. I try to hold my ground, but he pump-pushes me again and I feel as if his palms are going to cave in my chest. I stagger another step backward.

"Walter," I huff, "knock it off."

We're past the trial here and on to the sentence.

He hits me again. I take another step back, my shoe, sloshing down into soupy sand.

"Walter!"

He comes at me again. I step backward, this time to avoid the blow. He lunges, off balance, momentarily. His face is maroon. His eyes bulging, glistening. He charges at me, drives his shoulder into my mid-section, again, lifts me off my feet and body-slams me down, on my back, in the shallow water. A wavelet slaps ice-cold

216

against my cheek. Walter is sitting on me, his knees on my biceps, his hands around my neck. He is pushing my head into the wet sand, squeezing his hands. The back of my head compresses sand until the water level is about half-way up my cheeks. Walter is pushing and at the same time squeezing, trying to get my face under water. He can't seem to make up his mind whether to choke me or drown me.

"Whahllta!" I gasp.

I jerk my right knee into the small of his back. It pushes a beerie-scented blast of air out his mouth. His hands loosen. I gasp, breathe in a mixture of air and sea water, rasp a constricted cough. His hands tighten again. I drive me knee into his back again. Again, a blast of air. This time a string of spittle dribbles over his puffy lower lip. He sucks in a gulp of air, then exhales a blather of white froth. His hands loosen. I kick him again. He is gurgling. His eyes are bulging. His face turning beyond purple, moving to blue-black. I kick him again. He falls forward. His face against mine. Now he is rasping. It almost sounds like "help." I push him off me, stagger to my feet. Walter is lying face down in the water. I step over him and slosh out onto the beach. The undertow sucks him out a few yards. Fuckin' bastard. Wore himself out. Shouldda had a fuckin' stroke or somethin'. I am spangled in wet sand, spitting dead-fish water and grit. I am soaked, through to my wallet. I am fighting to catch my breath, tensing for the next assault from this Walter, this common . . . man, enraged at my accommodating his less-than-common wife. Fuck him. Fuck his wife. I am outraged.

He is lying face-down in the tide-swill. Limp as a used condom. I study this scene for a moment. I consider going to his assistance. I dismiss it. Fuck him. And fuck

217

his wife. I climb the breakwater, then walk out onto the road.

The grey Lumina is parked alongside the greased-black garbage drum. Garbage. Garbage. The driver's side door is open; the engine running. There is no physical stimulus, but I see it inside my guts: the dangling death-stick, the knotted-rope nose, the skeletonized skull, the arms like two semaphore flagpoles. As I pass the drum, I see two crushed beer cans atop. Two maraschino cherries atop a black-and-white sundae. The icing on the cake out in the rain. Where are you, you scavenging fuck? Come forward; show yourself. I think about releasing the brake on the Lumina, but it would only roll a few feet into the re-taining wall. He is back in the trees, seeing. He is praying I leave without damaging his car, without hurting him. I don't give a shit about him, and his kind. Walter and his kind. Me . . . and my kind.

Bottom-Feeder.

Bottom-Farmer.

Bottom-Food.

I am decomposing seaweed floured in grit, ambula-tory in a physical sense and back on course pro vita sua. I am. I am.

He will be disposed of, there is no doubt. I can theorize how, but choose not to. I am driven to act.

I grab hold of the chain-link fence and pull myself up. The metal diamonds are not conducive to gripping nor to more than a toehold. I pull and slip my way to the top, then over. I am unconcerned about anyone seeing me. As I approach the cage, I note the raccoon's eyes following my movements. They seem unconcerned, a drowning, arm-weary beetle, over the hump of fear, accepting.

I am at the cage, but have no idea how it was sprung or how to unspring it. I grab hold of what looks

218

like a gate. The raccoon swipes at my fingers and, with his claws, opens a knife-slice across the knuckles of my right hand. They've been known to carry rabies. I wonder if you can get it from a scratch. Isn't it something in the saliva?

I study the cage. Actually, it's a simple latch affair, which can only be actuated from the outside. I approach again. The raccoon raises a paw, again to strike. I grab the latch. The animal is clawing at me, frantically, but cannot reach me, because, this time, I've anticipated his strike.

I am a blank here. I don't know
what I did or what happens next.
I may have blacked out, but I don't
think so. The cage is empty now.
The animal is gone and there
is blood caked on one of my hands
from an old wound, which I don't
remember was there nor know where
I got it, nor remember if I care.

As I turn from Sound Beach Road onto my block, a village police car is heading in the direction from which I've come. He does not seem to be in a hurry. Through the open window I eavesdrop a crackled "trespass," for which I will seek no forgiveness.

63

They leave in the morning for the office, but never return. The sky falls down on them. I have orphaned the wife and kids, left them without the principal wage-earner. Without giving it a thought. My thoughts are about my-self. Every day, every step I take crushes to death count-less plants and animals. Most of my victims I never see (like a napalm strike on a Cong village), but I know they are there. I don't want to leave the apartment. I don't want to kill anymore. I can't. Thou shalt not kill. If thou walkest, thou shalt kill. It's all fucked up. I mean it's re-ally all fucked up. Isn't it?

"I murdered him."

"You said you were defending your own life."

"I was, up until the point when I'd gotten him off me and he was gurgling and inhaling water."

"The man was trying to kill you. You wanted to es-cape. Going back may have placed you back in harm's way. You cannot be faulted for inaction."

"I *wanted* him to die. His death was a solution to a perplexing problem, one I may not have been able to solve."

"He came at you."

"He felt he had a good reason."

"And you? Did you?"

"No. He should have killed Ruth. She was his wife."

"Do you mean that?"

" . . . Of course not. The man was a hypocrite. He was denying his wife the very thing he was enjoying himself. But if he were going to kill anyone, he should have gone after Ruth."

"Well then, what is your problem here?"

"Why are you doing this? You know very well what I'm struggling with. This is not about Walter and it's not about Ruth. This is about me. I was the only one who was there, the only one who could have gone to his aid . . . and I did not."

"Devil's advocate."

"What?"

"I'm playing devil's advocate. That's what I'm do-ing here."

"It's a new role for you."

"No. The devil and I go way back."

She is not looking at me. There is no telltale hint at sarcasm.

"This is uncharacteristic of *you*, Max: the pangs of guilt, the struggle with conscience. What is happening with you?"

"I'm lost, Aaley, hopelessly adrift."

"Hope? Hope is no help when you are adrift. Hope is weakness. Strength comes through understanding, direc-tion through knowledge, knowledge through . . . "

She breaks off. But, I know. I know. I see it clearly, for an instant, then it is gone. But it is there for me to recall. I own it. I'll recall it when I can.

"God help you, Max."

"God? He has his own problem."

"What do you know about God? What do you care?"

"You brought it up."

"It's an expression, Max."

"That's the problem, Aaley. *This* is an expression. All this. He created this mess. This whole fucking thing is

221

here because *He* has a problem. He lives in ecstasy, but ecstasy is a comparative sensation. It cannot be sustained. It can only be experienced in doses and then only as compared to the absence of ecstasy. Nothing interesting is sustained in perpetuity; the mind numbs to the sensation. God created the universe because He was bored. Its sustained perfection lapsed into numbness, so He disrupted it. Then He grew envious because His fallible creatures could experience true ecstasy. Now, God just wants to get laid . . . but that is not an experience for the infallible. So ecstasy has been commandeered by Satan. So the real battle, like everything else in the universe is going on inside the mind of God. Everything -- all this shit -- is just a figment of His imagination. Good and evil are battling for God's attention inside His mind. And, at this point, evil is winning."

She smiles. I'm bullshitting her and she smiles. I can't remember when she has smiled.

"What?" I ask.

"You're blaming God for all the shit you've pulled?"

"Why not?"

Her smile broadens. I love it.

"What?" I ask again.

"I don't *know* what. *You* have to take it from here. You have to lead the way."

"I see."

"Yes."

We are quiet for a moment, then, "I'll join you," she takes up.

"Even though you don't know where I'm going?"

"Yes, of course."

We are quiet again.

"Who is Margaret Montgomery?"

"She's dead."

222

"Who was she, then?"

"Imaginary. A momentary disguise, during a time of uncertainty."

I probe her eyes with mine.

"Dead," she says, emphatically.

64

"You murdered him."
I don't answer.
"I know it was you."
I was defending my own life.
"You don't have to answer me, Max. I know it was you."

> *The man was trying to kill me. I wanted to escape.*

"He told me he was going to get you, Max. They called me and told me they found his body lodged among the rocks of the breakwater, where you go for your smoke. They'd had a call from someone who would not leave his name. They said he had a stroke and drowned, but I know you hang out there. I know you killed him."

> *He came at me.*

"Well, what should I do about this, Max? You know I can't just let this alone. I mean I have to do something, right?

> *He should have killed you.*

I drop the handset back into the cradle.
I have to do something.

> *Yes, I suppose you have to.*

Some sins of the past develop lives of their own. Once you give birth to them, they set off on courses of their own. My sin with Bags is out there wandering free in space, an ever-present danger with a life apart from the one I would have chosen for it, from the death I had willed it.

65

"I need some time in the city, interact with people who could give a shit less about me and my past. I need to dissolve in humanity for a while."

"You're referring to the apartment."

"I'll pay rent, clean up before I leave."

"Just go. I have a woman who cleans once a week."

"Thanks."

"Come back whole. Rediscover who you are."

"Thanks, anyway."

66

The alley tree lifts its centripedal paws in the persistent breeze, the undersides of its palms a survivor's pale green, fading to white in the flat light. I have an inexplicable attachment to the alley tree, its insistence upon the spot it has staked, an illegal alien gripping tenaciously to a position none of the natives wanted until the alley tree had demonstrated its viability. The flailing branches of the ailanthus, that grows from a square of earth opposite her front door, are terrifying to Aaley, feigning a paw-pet, then clawing with the approach of fresh flesh. There is a mutant quality to the city tree she finds upsetting, a juxtaposition she finds flawed.

"When they wave the branches of the city tree," she says, "you should (have) run."

"I cannot turn from the city," I answer. "It is the locus of congregation, in effect the audience."

"Then dodge and weave and keep them off balance."

"I will not tell lies."[1]

"That hadn't stopped you in the past."

"That was then."

"Then I . . . cannot do what I hate."[1] The sadness informs her eyes.

"What?" I ask.

"I want to know more about your father."

"How can you do that?"

"Through loving you."

"My father is dead."

"So you've told me."

"You don't think so?"

226

"No."

"On what evidence?"

"A sense of foreboding. His influence can be destructive."

"He has no influence."

"Totally destructive."

"So why pursue him?"

"I need to know."

"Know what?"

"I don't know."

67

SLOW DOWN A BIT IT'S NOT TIME

Agency causes only occasional disruptions. He flicks the clock a bit. It jettisons a spark. The corrosive stays hidden deep within.

The story pieced together from interviews with those who had witnessed it and from the results of medical reports, went like this.

Dr. Victoria drove her Mercedes down the entrance ramp, slid lane by lane to the left, then notched herself into the HOV lane. It was the thick of the afternoon rush. Her female beagle, Abercrombie, was in the familiar position on the front passenger seat, paws on the dash, eyes affixed on events beyond the windshield. The road signs clearly indicated that the lane was for vehicles transporting two or more passengers, but the Vickster applied to herself only those rules which worked to her benefit. If stopped by the police, she simply showed her hospital ID, declared she was on her way to a medical emergency and, if the officer persisted in his or her questioning, she would become angry, declare that someone's life or future well-being was hanging in the balance and that "you, Officer Dolan" would be held personally responsible for the tragic outcome. It worked every time. The delay with the policeperson would inevitably erase any time she had gained by insinuating herself into the faster lane, but wherever there existed the trappings of privilege or preferential treatment, the Vickster appropriated them for her own. That *was* the greater reward.

They could only speculate what had caused her to dart from the HOV lane across the striped divider -- a last-second decision to head for an exit, a sudden distraction caused by Abercrombie, falling asleep at the wheel . . . all speculation -- but the movement was so abrupt the driver of the fuel truck could only manage a sudden swerve in the opposite direction. The move jackknifed the tanker and rolled it atop the Vickster's Mercedes, flattening the car's passenger cabin to a frisbee and killing woman and bitch instantly. At least that was what those who didn't know her hoped had happened, because the friction of metal against concrete exploded the tank full of gasoline, incinerating the occupants so totally it took more than twenty-four hours to determine the driver's sex, before they could be certain that the driver was, in fact, Dr. Victoria. For an entire day after the positive ID, staffers of the OB/GYN Department muttered to each other, "poor Abercrombie; what a way to go." For weeks and months after that, the words coalesced into a kind of real victory slogan: "Poor Abercrombie. Poor, poor Abercrombie."

68

"Daddy?"

I awake with a start. My head snaps forward. I have been dozing in my chair with my legs on the corner of my desk. My daughter, Sarah, is standing alongside. She is frightened. A beam of terror cuts through me. Then I realize it is I that has caused her fear.

"I did not want to disturb you, but . . . "

"It's O.K.," I say. "You startled me. I'm sorry if that frightened you."

Her eyes soften, momentarily, then retrieve a bit of fright as she now must address why she has disturbed me.

My God, what has become of my humanity? Did I ever really have any?

"May I read you something?" she asks. "It's due tomorrow."

Read me? . . . It's better if I see it on paper. But she wants to read it to me. She is proud of it.

It's a book review of a novel by a pop author, one of the better of a bad lot, and one of her favorites. She reads. It is a mediocre piece. And I am tempted to critique it tightly, but now, of course, sit on the horns of a dilemma. Why did she decide to read this to me? Was it her mother's idea? It is for an English class, but Sarah has always been quite vocal about how much she hates to write and read all "that boring stuff" you read in English class. Obviously, she likes what she has accomplished and has decided to risk the ultimate confrontation, or . . .

With this one bold stroke, she is calling into question so much that I have been so sure of. Suddenly, the positive reaction of a junior high school English teacher has significance. I want a good grade. If I choose to offer constructive criticism, it will be my grade as well. If I am less critical than the piece warrants, my grade may be lower . . . Shit, it's *her* work. A report on a piece of crap writing. How much can I reasonably expect? If I say it's fine and she gets a low grade, my stature with her will sink lower. Can it get lower? You bet your ass. Shit, assess it in terms of what it is, in terms of its audience. Why am I doing this? Breaking the laws.

She is looking at me again, sadness now tempering the enthusiasm that informed her reading.

"It's very good, Sarah," I say, finally. "I have some suggestions you may want to consider."

She listens intently while I show her how to better manage the flow of her argument, now to strengthen some sentences. I am wound up; into this. It is coming together. I am going overboard. " . . . But I never stop editing, rewriting. You know how I am." She doesn't have a clue. Why should she? I am terrified to take my eyes from the paper that now is my refuge. But, of course, I must.

Her eyes are ablaze. "Yes, daddy," she says, excitedly, "I see. Yes, this would be much better. That would work better."

What is going on here? I need to stop. I cannot go further. I would take control. It would ruin everything. Ruin what? I stop. Opt for a B. It is what must be.

"Thank you, daddy, thank you. I'll fix it."

"It's not broke, Sarah. They're just . . . suggestions. You did well. I just . . . I always make changes. You don't have to."

"But I will. Thanks."

She leaves . . . only her aura. No worms. No maggots. Daddy's little girl.

It is too late to deal differently with my children. They are their mother's. To try to reclaim even a measure of their attention would unground them. Oomieka has prepared them for a world with which I have had difficulty. I have no useful lessons to teach them. They are scientists, not poets. I decide the best I can offer is to keep my temper and my distance. It is a positive decision in favor of negative space. The only disappointment . . . is mine. How odd.

69

Oomieka is in a trance. I want to say, well, you got your wish, but I sense it a shamelessly crude, even cruel, remark. I have twinges of pain, even remorse, when I think of The Vickster's end, but, like the others, I find the sentiment quickly shifts to the dog. Another of The Vickster's innocent victims.

Oomieka's life has been returned to her and that, to put the positive spin on it, is really what she had wished for. We are back on track. Life goes on.

"I'm leaving you, Max," she says. "Or should I say you're leaving me?"

"What are you talking about?"

"My life. It was commandeered, for a while, then returned. I cannot waste any more of it. With you, I waste too much of it. I can't do that."

"It's called a relationship, Oomieka. In a relationship, some time is expended on making the relationship work."

"Work? We don't work."

She's doing a variation on the trance, the deeply contemplative look.

"Yes," I say. "You've been through a bad period, but that's over now. I've had some problems, too--"

"I don't want to deal with them, your problems. I'm tired, Max. I don't want to spend time and energy on the relationship. I have other things I need to do."

"And the children?"

"What about them?"

"What *about* them?"

I look at her questioningly. I am groping here.

233

"The kids? Do you even remember their names?" she resumes.

"Give me a hint."

"You're a shit, Max."

Curdled cream coats her eyes.

"No, Oomieka, I'm not. I am who I am. And I am not a shit."

"Then why haven't you attended to your responsibilities, minimal though they are?"

"Look, Oomieka, people . . . you, the kids . . . people see things differently than I do. They measure . . . let's call it progress, in human time."

"Max, please, not your convoluted philosophy."

I ignore the comment, continue. "But, while people see each generation as gaining more knowledge than the previous one, all they discover is that the universe is more complex."

"MAax!"

Aa?

"Therefore, why should I give a shit about the future of beings who know less than I do?"

"They're your children, Max."

It's working. I've diverted her attention.

"I've had to work to house, feed and clothe them," I continue, "instead of doing what I needed to do."

"And I? I just let you struggle along earning a living, while I spend *your* money."

I answer with sorrowed eyes.

"They're your children."

"No! No one is anyone else's child."

"I don't even know what that means."

I've fucked with my own strategy and now I'm losing her again.

"It means--"

234

"You're a shit, Max."

I sigh. "No, Oomieka, I am not."

She is staring at me, her cheeks reddening, her eyes narrowing, a brawler. She shakes her head. "Get out, Max," she says.

"Excuse me?"

"No, Max, I will not. Get out."

"Get out?"

"Get out. Go. Leave." She fixes me in her gaze. "Go to her."

"Her?"

"Oh, please."

"This is not about some . . . 'her.'"

"Leave me, Max. We are a mismatch. I know it. You know it. Anyway, it doesn't matter."

Now I am shaking my head. "I love you, Oomieka. I truly do."

"Not enough."

"Not enough? Love?"

"No. You are bound for self-destruction. I cannot help you and that offends everything I represent. I have things I need to do. You are a terrible distraction. Go."

The streets again? The streets are my pathway to . . . . My sorrow is immense, intense, without sense. It is crushing me. It is my death. It is approaching. I must pass through it to get wherever I am going. Wherever the f___ I am going. F___. No word. A non-word. Fffff___. I am crushed. Crashing. Shrinking. Bowed. Beaten. I need to hide, but where? In the circle of my own shadow. But I cannot remain immobile. I must move. I am in motion. In . . . transit. I am enroute. I am. I am. I am not . . . . I am not the embodiment of evil. My life was commandeered . . . then returned. *I am your connection.* I am

235

someone who has lost his way. Too easy. Too simple. Too . . .

Do I take my clothes?

She has not shown me to the door. She is on the sofa watching her soaps and doing her needlepoint. I show myself to the door.

Do I ask myself to leave?

I exit. Start up the Z, turn down Sound Beach Road. Do I go back for my clothes?

Why do I even give a shit about my clothes? My life as I've known it for the past three decades is over.

Over?

Oh, it's over, Jack.

The saddest thing of all is that suddenly it occurs to me that I have loved Oomieka, truly loved her. She . . . she is not . . . my connection. We are in intersecting orbits from different dimensions. We are an intersection out of synch. She cannot stop in my dimension. There is no pause for us. No stasis. We have a distinct past because it is something we have fashioned. We would have charted a future similarly, artificially. But during our time together I grew to love her. As we scripted our past, prescribed our future. This . . . living together had its elements. Her face. I have always loved her face. Even watching it grow old, blotching, creasing, greying, I have loved her face. The sound of her voice. The smell of her skin . . . along the nape of her neck, behind her ear. Her confidence, her self-assuredness. Where I have none. Where I cared not a wit about such shit, but admired it, nonetheless in her.

Oomieka had created a social structure designed to relieve me of my existence, the individuality-bordering-on-madness that had blossomed when my husbandless mother had failed to provide me with the protective circle I'd required as a child to deliver me from fear. But now, I

236

worked the perimeter of Oomieka's circle and crossed inside only during moments of unbearable anxiety, then to spring from it raging about even the temporary loss of identity; clutching about frantically to recover the fear that provided the impetus which kept me in motion.

"How can I continue to abide your insistence on dying?" she'd say. "And don't answer, 'we all die.'"

"But not until it's time," I'd answer. "And it's not time."

It had never occurred to me that fear was a major component in the way Oomieka dealt with life: more specifically, fear of the unknown. She needed the predictability of the happy endings of her trashy novels, the needlepoint designs she can see clearly on the packaging. My monologues invariably led from the real *to* the unreal, for Oomieka a reverse flow from the solution to the problem.

So why did she marry me? Or, more to the point, why did I marry her?

Because she was a woman who could resist me? And I could not resist that.

The saddest thing of all is that I loved Oomieka, truly loved her. Despite all my infidelities, I have grown more in love with her with each passing day. I know it sounds absurd. But she is right. This is a habit thing. A comfort zone, a love story nonetheless. But, I am not her connection. If I am not, who is? Does she have one? Has she found him and managed to keep that from me? I think not. Her patients are where she connects. It is an indistinct connection, a circuit which can be broken. For years, I was her perpetual patient. But that relationship has been a weight around her neck. She has been selected as one of the warriors and she has spent far too much of her time trying to rescue my ass. At the expense of others. And I accepted it. Enjoyed it. Diverted her. Like The Vickster.

So, do I need my clothes?

Ficus!

No.

Ruth,

hovering,

somewhere.

My mind blanks: the pulled cotton swab, the inside of a cloud. A metal point pierces the Z window near my left temple and lodges in the glass. Loosens. Drops out. Disappears without a trace. I drive on.

I am with Oomieka at the Baie des Anges in Cap d'Antibes with the wind ruffling her close-cropped, jet-black hair. I see my young face in the sheen of her dark green glasses and a shiver runs through me. For that brief moment, I was freed to love the earth. And then she said what she said about how I needed to conduct myself and I could never capture what I had for the instant I lived in the reversed image of her dark glasses. But it somehow managed to live on, behind the screen of my vision, like a sublimated virus hiding along a ganglia, under continual assault from antidotes, but never killed dead. So, yes, the saddest thing is that I loved Oomieka . . .

I find a space two blocks from Aaley's place. Pace. Then home. The dwellings: stone tombs, boulders rolled against the exits. No admittance to a hostile universe. No exit to the fearful humans within.

I am the host in transit. A ghost in quest of a string of words. The words, grown too complex. The formula out of control. A useless language. But it's all I have. For now. The here and now. The where and when. A patchwork of russet fields at the edge of the forest; broken, frozen stalks splattered in birdshit. You have to look at the landscape, step back and look at the entire work. Cubist. Multi-multi-dimensional. The single pattern. The clock without hands. The hand without clocks. A trickle of cola-colored liquid diverges around an icecube melting in a polluted, lowing sun. Cleansed atoms. A treetrunk streaked in dog piss. No. The point of impact is too high.

I arrive. Still alive.

I turn and mount the stair.

(My hair, in the glass, has, in fact, grown thin.)

What is the shape of a perfect stair?

Do I care?

Do I care?

I care?

I mount the stone steps. Mount the stone . . . The stone is eroding, cracking, turning to powder. To sand. Aaley, help. Hhhhelp me.

I can't help you anymore. You're on your own.

Who's there? Who's here?

She is at the door. Wide-eyed. She looks drugged. No, in some kind of trance.

Max, wait here. She points me to the sofa.

Don't move.

No matter what.

She disappears behind the door. I go pour. This is my blood. This is my . . . corruption. I am decayed, decaying, about to decay. I am putrefied, putrefying, putrid. I drink . . . my blood.

The lights brown down, flicker out for a second's fraction, return to brown, shit brown, polluted air layered over the city.

A cry, a pitiful whine, transmigrates the pine. The wall thins to film: her breasts are bloodied by serpent bites. I make no move to rise, with legs or otherwise.

239

A cry, a doleful, basso groan, falls and crawls beneath the door. Her vulva bitten by fangéd heads.

Once more, I do not rise.

A cry, a middletonal note, the throat bumps against the door. She is squatting, legs akimbo, a gaping, endless tunnel between, leading far back into a nether world.

Again, I sit. No, I am no shit.

A creecry flies. Demons take torches to her skin. She is rimmed in flame, drops prostrate, raises her arms and begs for strength. And now I note the light's reply.

A crawling, clawing cry and I am frozen in fear. The demons fan the flames. The light brightens further, presses near.

A cry, a shriek. Demons blow the flames white hot. I cannot rise, my knees too weak.

A cry, inaudible but there, and I and I . . . and I . . . have lost my rhyme, in a room awash in rays, shafts and spots and rivers and splashes in dots and . . .

I rise at last at some wordless bidding. The door creaks open and she emerges. Her face a circle of liquid light. She's wrapped in ice, a mist of miniature crystalline globes atomisized falls about her from the greenglow of a mossclothed cliffcave. She steps from the resumed room.

Her body is misted, as if emerging from a forest laved in a cloud. Her hair is soaked, flattened against the sides of her head, tendriled to her breasts, dripping perfumed pellets to puddles at her feet. Light runs in rivulets around her contours, in random passages down the ovum of her stomach, collecting in salted groupings of stars sprinkled about her pubis. She exudes spices of the east, pungent petals of plants that are less than memories. Her eyes beg me to hold her. I tremble in fear, pure and unencumbered. This is a new experience. I don't know what to make of it. She is there. I am still here.

240

Tears glisten on her face.
Woman, why do you cry?
She does not reply.
With trembling fingers, I
thin the tears across her cheeks.
You are with me nowandforever.
"God, you are so beautiful."
I can't get over the radiance. It is not even visible.
It's just there. I wonder if it's always been there. I'm sure
it has, but I was unaware of it. It's senseless.
"You make me feel so good."
"And you me."
I want to remain here forever, in this space, in zero
time. What excuse can there be to leave? My mission?
This is my mission: this room, in zero time.
But you are not here yet.
I know. I need to get out, to enter the city. I ask
her to come with me, for now I am afraid.
She says the harm that comes to me in the city is
ephemeral.
I say the thing I fear is me and what I am choosing
to be . . . come. Come. Come. It is a new element. Re-
newed element. The renewal of an ancient invitation.
come lets wash
She takes my hand.
She leads me to the white porcelain basin, removes
with delicate hands my clothes and laves me head to feet.
When she is finished, I do the same for her.
She is toweling off her face. Now, I am aware of
an irritation. It looks like a scab, blackened by the atmosphere, affixed to the hard surface of my left quadriceps. I
pull a kleenex from a box atop the toilet tank and reach to
wipe the blot away. It is affixed to two hairs. The hairs are
waving at me.

241

"Aaley!"

She turns abruptly, removes the towel from her face. I point to the spot.

"Don't move," she commands, removes a tweezer from a drawer in the vanity below the sink. "I must get it all," she mumbles as she positions the tweezer blades, right against my flesh, on either side of the invasive demon. She applies pressure. The legs beat frantically in air. She pulls the beast backward, until the head is extracted, then she grips the skull in her miniature vice.

"Kill it!" I cry. "Kill it before it spreads!"

She cracks its skull, then drops the body into the tissue and stuffs the tissue into a paper cup.

A white-cored welt has erupted around the point of extraction, a blue dot of oxygenated blood at its center.

"We'll monitor it," she says, "for signs of infection."

I stand, a bit, in awe.

I'll pour some wine

She takes again my hand, our fingers weave.

this is my blood

The work begins renewed.

We lay down together, but it is not like before. I am pressed against her. She is wearing a short, pink night-gown. Earlier, when she stood before me, it offered tantalizing hints of her beautiful physique. I embraced her and nestled my face in the curve where her neck joins her left shoulder. I pressed my lips against her skin. I wanted to taste only her taste and nothing else, ever. I inhaled the ambrosia of her flesh. It is the smell that moves me. In bed, her gown has ridden to her waist, exposing her beautiful haunches. My penis nestles between her buttocks, but it is not the independent warrior it once was. The smoothness of her skin entrances me now; that touch that humbles velvet. It is her smell that holds me fast to her. I want to stay, pressed together like this, a single wafered being, forever. I synchronize my breathing to hers, then listen. Her breathing is the soft breath of the wind. The sound is heavenly. I want to breathe my breath through her, inhale her exhalations. The soft breathbreeze.

She has become everywoman. She is at once my-lover, mymother, mysister, and now, for all intents and purposes, mywife. She has assumed the radiance. The grunge is leaving our relationship, but not without protest, not without strips of my flesh under its fingernails. And, there is this sense of Ruth, circling, the silent scream hugging the perimeter.

kill it

kill it before it spreads

I will have to make decisions, rapidly, within a context I have not known for many years. But now it is this change in Aaley that is having the most profound effect upon me. This tenderness. It has eroded the sensuality. Replaced it. I am being sucked to it, but I don't *want* to give up the grunge. I don't know if I can. I enjoyed it. A lot. But there is now an enfolding quality to her. I just want to be wrapped within her. Fitted within her. To become part of her and she of me.

She rises on her left elbow, touches my face with the palm of her right hand, her fingers bent back so they do not come in contact with my cheek. Her palm is like a silken pillow in a sultan's tent. She brushes it back and forth across the surface of my skin as if in a ritual of affection. The palm at the end of the mind.[1] It is an obeisance to the transformation, an ascent to a higher place, a place with its own brand of dangers. Like Esteban and the museum, I now have something to lose. It was not supposed

243

to be that way. I have lost the center, to the circle that sur-
rounds it. Elohi. Elohi. Lama. Shebaqtani?

"Do you forgive me?" she asks.

"Yes, of course."

"As I forgive you."

"Divine."

She smiles. It is an illumination.

"I will not lose you. This time."

There is no time.

Something is different. This time. I am inside a
tunnel. A snug, accommodating tunnel. The warm scarf
protecting my neck from the cold atmosphere. I am welcome here. I feel it. I feel welcome here. She has a need,
an ancient need, and I fulfill it. It is my welcome. But, beyond that she wants me here. She has asked me in by invitation. Her skin is different, the body covering she wears
like a kit-skin glove a micron thick and brushed smooth.
She sighs her breathperfume. It is a sweet chemicalized
swoon. Her hair smells of dried sweat the way autumn
grass exchanges body fluids with the blue-white wind. I
am comfortably aware of the soft white touch of her belly
against mine. The mine. What is happening here, without
fear? The nouns are the same, even if I resort to syno-
nyms, the euphemisms. But the adjectives are different.
The verbs. The metaphors. They are for the most part unexpressed. Words, without words. But I need words. I
work in words. They define me. They are me. I am nothing without words. Nothing.

I release inside her, at the far end of the tunnel. It is
a surprise. I did not know it was coming until it came, but
all the same . . . it feels warm, just warm, well warm. An
ignition that does not burn. Unrapid oxidation. A lone
atom of oxygen. A single breath for a micro-organism.
She is warm. Inside and out. Perfect warm. 72°. She is

244

surface, inside and out. Suddenly there is no depth, only surface. It is a glorious thing to experience. I am lying on top of her, motionless. Her, too. I don't know what I feel. I need to move to know what I feel. I don't want to move. I can't move. But I feel. I just don't know what it is . . . that I feel. Different. I feel different. Different from what? I need a baseline. Compared to nothing. I want to compare it to nothing. That's the difference. I feel different compared to nothing. Not nothing as in zero. Nothing as in anything else.

I am at the window, watching the firelight converge to a thin line beneath the pyramid atop the stone structure across the plaza in the blackness. Below, black crows clear the streets of roadkill, the remnants of pigs and cows and chickens and monkfish and homeless people.

On a mountain curve, a dump truck spits out a huge boulder and I am killed instantly.

I am emptied. Behind me the soft breathbreeze respirates. It is all that remains of mylife. It is all there is am   are. I am. You are. *Amare.* I am at the window, the city still asleep in   darkgreyblue, the golden staff amid, against a mount not there but here.

In the rust-colored mountains, God dragged his fingers across the red rock and created layers of green.

Transfixed am I on a burning crystal on the stone ledge, a fourpointed star, an X standing on one leg, it burns out, burns into the emptiness. Tempt not he said and stood. A single star in the black too. Never should have doubted. Never *really* doubted. Should have cared. Shouldhave-cared.

awake
yes
you sleep
don't know

mm
i have to go
yes
ill be with you later
ill come
i know
i no
I/O
1/0.

70

Carpentry

Paradise
(I've measured twice)
is half an inch from hell.

71

To avoid roadkill, I will take the train. I place a
buffer between me and those who this day must die. So
that I may live. Why is it that in the overall scheme of
things, *some*thing must die, so that I may live?

Paper-thin circles emanate from drops of rain falling from the roof of the station house into the puddle at my
feet. The drops explode, the circles form, then dissipate.
The whool of the whaal in the wheel of the whorl.[1]

A group of smokers is forming to my right. They
greet each other by name, one by one, light up. They've
been doing this, every morning, for years. They have the
same conversation they've been having for years. They
grow old in this setting, in these words, die. Their children
take their places.

*The coming of thir secret foe . . . which way shall I
fly . . . Infinite wrath, and infinite despair . . .* [2]

A woman exits the building, then takes a position
between me and the group. I have seen her before. Her
face could be a pleasant one if she ever smiled, but it has
assumed a defensive scowl to protect her space. But we
share this space, this time. We exist. We exist together.
We have never officially acknowledged each other's existence. It's absurd. I watch her. As a fellow being. She
watches for the train. It comes from my left. She is facing
toward me. She is looking through me. Her eyes brush by
mine. I smile, begin to say "good morn--" She looks
away. My lips, my jaw, my eyes are frozen within a word.
I await, that way, the train. The smokers mark my awk-
ward countenance. Hey, I don't say, it's mine. Say, they
don't say, we're ours. Touché.

Red lights flash. The barriers fall. The diesel
chuffs into the station. A door stops directly opposite me.
We have a winner. I grab a handhold, cold, wet metal, pull
myself up the stairs, roll back the door, hold it for the
woman who discounted me. Take a seat.

I am in car number thirty-six-sixty-six, a beat-up affair with mars, gouges, scratches and punctures in its hard-
plastic seatbacks and semi-hard-plastic seats. The
timetable schedules a ride of two hours and ten minutes,
with thirteen minutes to make a connection south of the
city, thirty-nine minutes into the trip.

Oomieka is well rid of me. I tell Aaley nothing.
I'm not completely sure how long I'll be gone. I pack only
a minimal assortment of clothes, take only a book of Wallace Stevens poems and a book-without-words. I buy a
pack of cigarettes at the station.

I am early to board so I have my choice of seats. I
take one on the right-hand side, facing forward -- so I can
see where I'm going, not where I've been. Over time, the
car fills in. An old man enters and takes a seat against the
front bulkhead on the left-hand side, facing backward. He
looks vaguely familiar. I scribble some notes about the
frontward/backward thing and a face from the past dis-
guised in creases and furrows. I replace creases and furrows with lines. Economy of words, minimalist if less
descriptive.

We jerk away from the station, leaving behind rusting cross-beams and piss-stained bricks. A pigeon races us
to the end of the platform, then alights on a metal cross to
pick at the eyeballs of a ghost. We enter a landscape of
oiled gravel and yellowing plant-stalks.

Suddenly, I am dying for a cigarette. I arise from
my seat, place one of my bags in its midst to save my place
and exit the car, taking up a position between the doors. I

ignore the no-smoking sign, light up and blow smoked
ropes into the slipstream. Almost immediately, I begin to
feel light-headed and await, thereby, some artistic inspiration to blossom in the ether. None comes. I take a few
more drags, study the green blur outside the train. I begin
to grow faint. I should toss the cigarette but I have two
drags-worth left. I take one of them, grow more faint. I
fall toward the opening on the left-hand side. I sense a
strong pull in that direction. Or maybe it's just the weakness in my legs. Or both. I take another drag. My vision
is going white. As night. There is perhaps one more drag.
I clamp my knuckles together. I will have it. I will. I have
gone from blurred grey shapes to snow-blindness. A white
cyclone with the vacuum sucking my legs. And then red.
A searing at the meat-pads amidst my fingers and I drop
the butt. The smell of hair-ash and singed flesh, a most unpleasant experience. But it has unsmoked my brain and I
regain my balance, return to my seat. I remove and stow
the bag, turn and lower myself into place. I am aware once
more of the lined face of the old man. He seems surprised
to see me.

　　　The green blur fills the windows through the burbs.
As we slow into the stations, the blur focuses into oaks, maples, sycamores, old, tall pines, choke cherries with their
mutant leaves and blade-leafed ailanthus, the palm tree of
railroad rights-of-way and dank alleys. Alleys. There are
many. Many, many. Aaley; there is only one. Only the
one. We visit, then leave stations flanked by parking lots
where cars align perfectly like beaded genes on a chromo-
some chain. We fly by too quickly for me to identify the
mutant strain. I extract from my pack the book of Stevens
poems: *The Palm at the End of the Mind*. I am reading it,
this time, from back to front. I want to see where he went,
then where he'd been.

250

The palm at the end of the mind
Beyond the last thought, rises . . .
A gold-feathered bird
Sings . . . without human meaning . . .
You know then that it is not the reason
That makes us happy or unhappy . . . [3]

It is a short poem, "Of Mere Being," only twelve
lines; a quartet of three-line stanzas. The last of a collection that takes the first line of this poem for its title. *End of
the mind. Without human meaning. It is not the reason
that makes us happy or unhappy.* It is *not* the reason. It is
not *the* reason. The palm stands on the *edge* of space. On
the edge of space. Space. Where is time? On the edge?
The same edge? Convergence? Not there? Has it ended
already? Was it ever there? Of *mere* being. To be is mere.
Is merely . . . what? A short poem. Part of a collection,
but standing alone. Only four triplets. Triplets. Why?
Why four? It took four stanzas to say it? Four has some
significance? My poem has no end. I've never thought of
it in terms of ending; getting somewhere. Poems don't
end. They grow, expand outward, growing continually
larger. Ever after. Until they converge? At the end of the
mind? At the end?

Four stanzas, neat, tidy, economical, say it all.

So we are heading due north now. Compass point
zero. Diversions to the east and west, of course, even one
that winds south for a portion of a mile to cross a mountain
at a less-demanding grade. We follow a river snaking
through a cleft, then resume our journey north through
small towns, in shaved places between green armpits,
named for colonial conquerors and defeated aborigines.

Sweet Thames run softly till I end my song,
Sweet Thames run softly, for I speak not loud or
long [4]

The green blur continues to accompany. It is a linear statement, with black shadows thinning as the velocity increases to become a musical staff sans notes: the non-accompaniment to my book-without-words. In the nihilistic monotony, my eyelids are gaining weight, falling closed, then springing upward to various sensory stimuli, but their general movement is in the direction of sleep and I drop off into a world of other small towns, at other small times.

I had a teacher once who kept insisting the world was mine for the taking. I had the raw intelligence, but I was worshipping at the wrong temple.

"This writing poetry is a very nice hobby," he'd said, "but a math-based career is where you'll make your money: science or finance or computers (an emerging field)."

Alas he'd played a significant role in my not following his advice. He was such a total asshole. And, I'd reasoned, if this was the sort of person I could expect to encounter . . . or become . . . Besides, money had never been a major interest for me. Although I can't quite explain why because pussy *was* an emerging interest and I could see money bought lots of it, if not directly, then indirectly.

"You just don't seem to get it," he'd press. He was one of those assholes who have to prevail. He didn't so much give a shit about whether I followed his advice or not, it was really more of a contest. He'd determined to achieve a certain outcome and I would not let him. "Jesus threw the money changers out of the temple and look where he ended up?"

"Where was that? In Heaven," I'd counter to further annoy him.

He'd shake his head and grumble because on other occasions, I'd been steadfast in my condemnation of the

252

doctrines of organized religion. A bunch of bullshit, I'd said.

"Someone will own the world," he'd insist, "and in this increasingly mathematically dependent universe, it will be those who prepare for the future, who grab for the gold ring. And I mean all of it: the mountains, the valleys, the rivers, Jerusalem, Rome, even Athens." (The cities he'd selected were modern ones, icons of the mathematically inspired industrial revolution, but in my poetic rendering of the universe, I'd opt for a more classical representation. In my case, if his offer were to have any allure, it would have to be thus.)

"Listen to me. I can give you all of it."

And he called himself a teacher. He was an imposter.

In the desires-based society that had been the result of our evolution to date (or the result of some ancient misdirection), all that mattered was what you were able to collect. He who has the most toys when he dies wins. But materialism was not my great sin. Sin was.

My teacher's face is still there trying to con me, jabbering away until it fades into the staff of green music, and he begins to sink into the verdant sludge, grasping at globs that cannot bear his weight, that cannot keep him from falling into the still-water darkness of a dead day.

A sunflower the size of a truck tire peeks in at my window as we glide into a station. It startles me as I return from my journey to high school. I jerk awake, kicking the seat in front of me and eliciting a grunted obscenity from the party occupying it. We sit a few minutes, quivering, then jerk forward and spurt upon our way.

The foliage is thinning. Even the ailanthus is stunted, widely spaced and anorexic, with drooping leaves the color of old motor oil. Scrub weeds fight with refuse for space. A major thoroughfare has joined courses with the railroad and hosts a mismatched procession of lumbering delivery trucks and hypertensed passenger cars, the flashing red barrier that protects our integrity knifing down before them, the difference between a second cup of coffee and a pissed-off supervisor. Razor wire coils across the tops of walls and fences, protecting manufacturing plants. Pieces of broken glass are embedded in the top of a brick wall around a Catholic church. Cast iron grates cover the doors of ramshackle residences. A dead cat has been pounded to cardboard by the press of traffic. Kudzu covers any remaining plantlife; an exotic plant taken out of context, blanketing the urban world; the paradise vine gone wild. What a life. What an existence.

I think about another butt break but decide against it because I am too lazy to get up and, for some incomprehensible reason, I am enjoying the view, the window framing my domain. *All this can be yours. Who the fuck wants it? It was beautiful once. Yeah . . . once.*

We slide into the mouth of the tunnel, a mechanized sodomy, just one of the daily gang bangs of trains, choking a city used to abuse. Light from the firmament shafts through grates in streams of grey, forming another particulate dance, that always, for me, transfigures the fall of bodies, this time to an underworld incarnate: hot metal squealing against metal, gaseous hissing, garbled conversation, atop the rapid purr of a great mechanical heart which, at that pace, simply cannot go on living. We stop just short of the platform, for no good reason. Or bad reason. Or any reason. Side light from the station triangulates an urban tablet just up ahead: "Fatso takes it up the ass." How could I feel anything but good about being back in town? Now where do I find this Fatso person?

254

When we are finally at the terminal, I hoist down my bags determined first to find a coffee shop where I can get some caffeine to go with another hit of nicotine. At the top of the ramp from the tracks is the local location of a do-nut franchise. I take a booth in the smoking section, order a glazed donut, coffee, and light up a smoke.

The old man from the train wanders in. He seems edgy, even a bit disoriented. When he sees me, he walks straight toward where I'm sitting, stops before the booth and asks if he "might have a word." (Actually, it sounded like he said "the word," but that makes no sense.) I don't want to talk to him but my other options would be rude, publicly rude. I nod for him to sit.

"I know we appear strangers," he says, "but I am sure we've met somewhere." The last word hangs, antici-pates a response.

Now ent'ring his great duel . . . though untried,
Against whate'er may tempt, whate'er seduce, Allure, or
terrify, or undermine.[5]

I say he looks vaguely familiar, but I don't think we've ever met, at least not socially.

He says he has had his wallet lifted and was left only with his return railroad ticket, which he'd tucked into his shirt pocket. Could I stand him to a couple of donuts, plain ones, little more than bread.

So shalt thou save thyself and us relieve With Food
[6]
. . .

He is lying. I can't say how I know, other than by instincts. This is some kind of scam, some kind of test. He probably has the wealth of the ages and just wants me to part with some of mine, do his bidding, succumb to his wiles. And, he has me at a disadvantage here. If I decline, I am telling a hungry old man no to less than a dollar's worth of donuts. If we have met, he has tried the same shit on me before.

He *has* tried this same shit on me before. He is *very* familiar. It's been the time factor that has dulled my memories.

"Where do I know you from?" I ask finally.

"Can't we discuss it over a cup of coffee and some donuts?"

"In a minute," I insist. "Where are you from?"

"Here and there, a bit of everywhere?"

"Try the here part."

"You know, no place in particular. Listen, can I call the waitress over?"

"Hold your horses. You must be from some place."

"No place you would have heard of."

"Try me."

"I travel. I don't stay put. I'm from every place, on my way to every place else -- "

"You're scamming me, aren't you?"

"Out of a buck's worth of donuts?"

"Stand up," I insist, my resolve hardening. "Empty your pockets onto the table."

"Who do you think you are," he snaps, "some kind of inquisitor, my judge and jury?"

"Someone who doesn't like to be bullshitted."

"Out of a few pieces of dough."

"Out of anything."

"Hey, fuck you," he snarls, rising from the seat. "I fought for lightweights like you. I did the dirty jobs, when no one else would, I smoked out the weaklings and showed them up for what they were. I greased the skids for dip-shits like you. I was serviceable to the powers that be."

256

"I'm sure whatever paths you traveled were those you chose," I answer maintaining my cool. "And I wish you good fortune with where you are headed."

"No you don't," he snaps back. "You want me to fall on my face."

"What you do, is your choice."

"Then you won't stand me to a couple of donuts?"

"This isn't about donuts."

"You will have to deal with me, or others like me. You will have to confront us. We will not go down easily." He turns and walks out of the shop, disappearing as if into thin air.

The black spot in the sky can bend light but cannot suck it in.

I finish my donut and my coffee and leave.

72

I surface from the underworld and its peculiar creatures, head toward the address Simeon has given me. It is in the better part of the city. How can he afford something like this on a teacher's pay? He must have beat it out of Guyana with a stash. Who knows what shit he pulled to get it?

Ahead is the mid-town cathedral, bathed in sunlight. The sun is striking with such intensity that I can see the silhouettes of women's bodies through their clothing. I feel I should turn away, but this is not an opportunity I've sought; it's been presented to me. Nonetheless, I avert my eyes toward the cathedral, where women in short skirts present an even-more-revealing view.

Am I to close my eyes? Is that what this is all about? Close my eyes. Is that what's right? What's right? What is wrong with what I am seeing? Can the virtuous man see unvirtuous things? Have I found the virtue in a cunt? Why not?

Simeon's apartment is on the thirteenth floor of a mid-town high-rise. He probably asked for the thirteenth floor. The building's entrance is a filigree of decorative bronze and brass, with gas lamp sentinels on either side of a gilded-glass door, swung open by a doorman who ushers me in to a security guard, who asks to whom I should be announced.

"I guess you'll have to announce me to me," I say.

He is unamused.

I show him a letter Simeon has given me, whereupon he checks a daybook and notes I am, in fact, to arrive today. He asks how long I'll be staying and I say I don't know. He looks at me askance and I almost answer the "hey, none of your fucking business" I withheld earlier, but simply repeat "I don't know," then add, "I'm doing some work, need a quiet place and this sounded like it was what I needed." He waves me through. I feel like saluting.

I cross the lobby, a green-marble-and-mirror affair with a fountain, the centerpiece of which is a nymph pouring water from a jug. She looks familiar. Perhaps we've had a relationship. "Friend of the bride," I murmur as I pass, press for one of three in a bank of elevators, the left one of which opens immediately and I ascend to my hermitage. The door opens into your classic bachelor pad. Simeon's wife has never been here. I don't get this. This is something on Simeon. It's not like him to allow any kind of advantage. And I am a particularly bad risk, with my status tenuous, or so it would appear. But he knows me better than that. This is not a game I play. It's his game. This is his way of showing me he is even better at *my* game than I am. Ah, but the joke is on him. I don't play that game any more. At least I don't think I do.

I walk to the window. The view from this height affords an odd perspective on the city. Most of the buildings in this the heart of town, the black heart of town, tower above my thirteenth floor perch. The claustrophobic gathering of concrete and glass is intimidating unless you recognize it for what it is: one of the ephemeral marks of man. Even here, where he appears in charge, here in the black heart of the city, even here, man cannot eradicate the presence of the universe. For below, through cracks in the sidewalk, the crabgrass and dandelion still grow, and somewhere, overhead, an osprey circles the piss-ant peaks, hunting small rodents for dinner.

I drop my bags near a dining room table, twist my book- without-words from a side pocket and scribble:

259

The apartments of close friends
have become preferable to home.
Short-term staging areas,
they are the arena of how far it can go;
how close it can come.

In the quiet light of a bed-table lamp,
time becomes
the line along the underside of her breast,
space
the world as seen through a patch of hair,
sense and non-sense
the smell of pheromones loosed
from a pile of discarded laundry.
These are irrational moments,
life reduced to the basics,
deplored by centuries of learned aversion.
It is the attraction.

In the apartments of close friends,
only the phlogiston remains
after the catch of the latch
and the sound of footfalls down the stairs
to the street,
into the flow of traffic
along the sidewalk.

I like this one. A lot. A Wallace Stevens, updated.
The drain of energy has left me weak. I remove my shoes
and lay down on the couch to nap. I awake restless. I need
to get out, but I am not hungry. I decide I will not eat, until
it is required. The thought of anything burnt or boiled, ani-

mal or plant, is repulsive. But I do not want to drink, either, at least not alcohol. I decide on coffee.

There is a new guard on duty, at the gate. But no doorman. Double duty. It is dark out. I tell him who I am, show him the letter. He says he's been told of my acceptable presence. It occurs to me I have not looked at my watch. It is twenty-three after midnight.

73

I've been dozing. I get off the couch and go into the bathroom where I splash cool water on my face. I pat my face dry with a hand-towel. I fix on the eyes in the mirror; they fix on me. I study me. Or me studies I. I lock on the eyes; and they on mine. Am I looking in? Or looking out? Is there anybody in there/out there?[1] I strain to look inside, but my defenses respond in kind. I strain further; they resist with equal force. There are fractional insights but I can't hold them, translate. I crack, drift to the cracks at the corners of my eyes, then outward to those that line the rest of my face. The eyes in the mirror lose interest.

What time is it? I should eat? I haven't eaten since the donuts, almost two days ago -- what, maybe forty hours? I've spent forty hours in a mid-city high-rise. Simeon's fuck pad. Shit, and he would deny me. Forty hours. How biblical. Forty days in the desert. Everyone spent forty days in the desert or someplace most people would rather not be. Why forty hours? A metaphor of course or, more accurately, a symbol for long, a long time. But there is no time. So that explains the zero, but what about the four? Why four zero? Why not five zero? Or seven? Or three? Or nine? Or one? Yeah, one. How odd. Four stanzas for "O Mere Being." A short poem. About a long time. There is no time. Now *that's* a long time.

Is my fast over? Does forty hours qualify? I'm starving. I need to blow this joint. I need to get out of this place, once and for all . . . time?

There is someone at the door.

There is someone at the door, but no one, except Simeon, knows I'm here. I am frozen, as if I have been caught at something, but I've been caught at nothing. Nothing.

Simeon would have called, let me know he was coming. Sure, it's his place, but he would have let me know he was coming. No one else knows I'm here.

It is a mistake. I will not answer. It will go away. The bell rings again.

And again.

And again.

And again.

I rise, approach the door. Just that and nothing more.

And again.

Fuck!

I reach for the knob.

And again.

Twist it. Hold that.

And again.

I open it.

Ruth.

She walks in. Talking. The sound of her voice trailing behind her like streamers in a Chinese parade.

"I'm your worst nightmare, Max. Something you beat down but who keeps coming back. Something you cannot repair, even if you had the balls to try."

How did you know I was here?

"I followed you, Max. I follow you all the time."

"You can't do that, Ruth."

"*You* are going to stop me?" she laughs.

"It's intimidation."

"You'll get an order of protection? Against the wife of your next-door neighbor? Your *dead* next-door neighbor?"

She is at the window, looking out.

"What do you want, Ruth?"

She turns, a grotesque smile bolted to her face. "I want to destroy you, Max: physically, mentally, emotionally, professionally, every 'ally' you can think of."

Ally? Think of Aaley?

"Why, Ruth?"

"You killed my husband, Max."

"No, Ruth. Not it. You want to destroy my world. Yes, Ruth, yes damn it."

She stares at me, searching for a read, a sign of weakness. Then she shakes her head, begins anew. "It's the use-and-discard thing you do, Max. I won't let you get away with it."

"And you've never done that yourself?"

"I invented it. I just won't let you do it to me."

I shake my head. "We . . . shared each other. I didn't use and/or discard you."

"Ah, but that's what's so satisfying about all this. It doesn't matter what *you* think, only what I think -- or do."

"That's not how it works, Ruth."

"How *what* works?"

"Life."

"Life?" She blurts out a laugh. "Shit, Max, you just don't get it, do you? *I* determine how life works. I do, not you. And I'm not going to stop until *I* destroy *you*."

"Why, Ruth?"

She studies my face and smiles again. It's an odd smile, not the evil sneer she's been wearing since she walked in. It's a kind of recognition thing. "It's something

I've *got* to do. Let's just say I'm driven. I'm evil. I just can't stop myself."

She is at the window again, her back to me, transfixed upon something. Without turning, she says, bouncing it off the glass, "come here."

I'm not in the mood for whatever trite metaphor she has found in the design of the skyline or the color of the sky.

"Why," she begins, "don't you opt to fly?"

"What?"

"Jump," she answers. "See if you can fly. It will be a much more pleasant way to die."

"What are you talking about?"

"Jump," she repeats. "Try to fly. You can do it. Show me you can fly. Then I will not have to make you die."

"Have you been drinking?"

"No!" she snaps. "Don't try to trivialize what I'm saying. Show me you can fly. You. The great one. Surely some angel will catch you and lower you gently to the pavement."

I pause. She means it. She's serious about this insanity. "You need psychiatric help, Ruth." I say it simply to answer something to her insane babble, but now she stares me down, her face as hard as a pagan sculpture.

"I'm not one of your silly little poems, Max. I'm your mortal enemy. And you made me what I am today."

This is crazy, this whole obsession with confrontation. Sure we had it out and I'd sent her back to live with Walter, down to her own personal hell, but it was not a hell of my creation, it had been a pre-existing condition. I am tired of taking the blame for it. Now *I* am angry.

"Go away, Ruth," I say sharply. "Leave."

265

"I want you to fly. I want to watch. Turn yourself into one of your poems and fly."

She has a stupid grin on her face, like she has created some clever theme and she won't let it go. But she has paused for a moment. She sees I am angry. She answers with sarcasm.

"Oh," she says, "what are you going to do, Maxie, take a swipe at me?"

"Don't tempt me," I say and I know the look on my face shows I mean it.

The smile drains from her face. She turns, opens the door, leaves it open, and walks to the elevator. She pushes the down button. The elevator comes and descendingly lighted numbers record her descent.

I need to go home, I decide. I have been out in this wasteland too long. It has not been a relief. It has been an ordeal. I need to go home.

266

74

A pause in the kinesis.
Redux red.
Leg elastic loose.
The past anchors me to the chair.
But I've been there. It's past.
It's present. I know things, now. I know what's
there. I know what it means. It's not what's there. I must
rise from the chair, mount the stair, escape (once and for
all) what's there. The rhymes are forced, albeit an attempt
at something clever, internally, but weak, very weak. Escape, however, is not the course. Never the course. Confrontation *is* the only way through this. The door. "Break
on through to the other side."[1] I cannot crumble. That is
past. Present replaces past. Becomes past. I feel alone, so
alone. I stare, over there. The pull is great. It is my great
weakness. Was. Still is. Was will not be. Is not was.

Aaley had seen it. She knew there was no known
substitute. So she took it on. Head on. She pulled it apart,
piece by sordid piece. She deconstructed me. And then --
only then - - she purged herself. She had scripted it. But it
was an anti-script. It was not   my   script. So how
could it be, if in fact, it was. Fact? There are no facts.

He does not know.

Holy shit! He   does   not   know. It wouldn't
be any fun for Him if He did. He rewrites the script as He
goes along, like they did for "Casablanca."

She rises to leave, glances my way. She smiles. I
return the smile. Spinagain.

75

I love the way the treetops wear the sunshine like a skull cap.

> *There's a certain Slant of light . . .*
> *Heavenly Hurt, it gives us -*
> *We can find no scar,*
> *But internal difference,*
> *Where the Meanings, are - . . .* [1]

I have managed an early train out of town. I am anxious to go home. I am traveling against the commute and I had anticipated the train would move quickly, but we are just chugging along: fits, starts, jerks and slow glides. Again, I am drawn to the landscape; you can't help it on a train. But this time the blur has been slowed to form distinctive shapes. It is remarkable, really. Nature via Emerson's transparent eyeball: I am nothing; I see all. [2]

The morning light breaks across trees in the oldest section of a cemetery, huge, old trees with crowns perfected over the decades, adding a branch here, a leaf there, to fill out round, or spear-shaped, or the squat flame atop a Christmas candle. Here the headstones are mottled and broken, their chiseled inscriptions long since erased by natural forces. The light, thrown sideways across the scene, casts striated shadows of grey upon the bright green grass. It's quite remarkable, really, this communion which comes with death. The good death. Here, the insects step on me. Here, I am chewed, spewed, pulverized and powdered, until I become part of the earth. The good earth. I guess there's a certain logic in the process, the preservation of matter, my reconstitution as a tree, but logic seems not the operative force here. And I draw comfort from the realization. Elements of the game are in my hands; the outcome is not. I don't think. I don't know. And there is a strange comfort in that as well.

> *Growth of Man - like Growth of Nature*
> *Gravitates within -* [3]

My God, what is happening to me. All this introspection, this reevaluation. Is it regret? No. I loved every minute of it. Love(d)? I want it back. I want Aaley back. The original Aaley. I want Oomieka back. I want the Aaley and Oomieka. That was the zenith. When I didn't have to choose. That was the zenith. Wasn't it?

Is it remorse. *God's institution? The Adequate of Hell?* [4]

The train jerks into a glide, accelerates slowly to the low end of its cruising range. I am going home, wherever that is; for now, whenever that is.

I feel like a space probe sent down here to collect data. Chicka. Chicka. Church in the early morning sunlight. Chicka. Chicka. Chi-- Smell of bread from the bakery down by the train yard. Chicka. Chicka. Chock. Rattle of a loose rod below the train window. Chicka. Channel of clear cool water falling over slick gray stones. ChickaChickaChock.

I have been trying to memorize "Of Mere Being," but I cannot. It is a mental thing. It is not the reason. It is only a few words in an order, arranged in the mind of another human being, another mere being, another dead being, but that is not the reason which makes us happy or not. The words are another failed attempt at discovering the message, cooked like a feather in a barbecue pit. A persistence of memory, left like a failed clock draped over a dead limb.

I escape the city with death in tow. It is merely a matter of time. I am wise to it now. I accept it. I can no

269

longer trod the earth. I understand my lack of suitability to
do so. Every step I take tramples to death . . . tramples to
death. My fangle-dangled wings are afire. It is why I have
crashed and burned. It was not the form but the content
did me in, not the method but the madness. Now, the aged
catalyst of my degeneration is the conjured agent of my resurrection. Elohi, Elohi, Aaley, Aaley, Bo-Baaley, Bo-
Nana, Bana, Fee, Fi, Fo, Faaley, Aaaaley.

Fuck you, Emily. That's undoubtedly what you
needed. It does have its therapeutic effects, you know. I
take up my journal and scribble:

. . . to a last hurrah - apologia pro vita sua

For Emily
Two thighs pure White - I focus on
My fantasy grows keen
Contrasting silky White, 'twas sure
A vulva lay between

Betwixt moistened hairs - I rode
My fantasizing on
Pushed aside Two pliant lips
And there - communed with God!

76

"Max, Max, why do you buck the system so? It seems hardly worth the energy. Is conforming so difficult? We all know the conformation is a lie."

"Let's just say I am who I am and I will not be relieved of my existence."

"O.K., Max, who are you?"

"I don't know . . . do you?"

"Know who I am or you are?"

"Either."

He is not amused.

I am. I smile.

"They'll crucify me. I've invested a good deal of my academic capital in your defense, Max, prepared the way for your resurrection."

Ah, Simeon The Biblical. "If we are employing inappropriately dramatic metaphors," I answer, "then you no longer have my cross to bear, Simeon. It'll be better for you in the long term, if you are shed of me."

He seems relieved, if unconvinced. The game is over. He will have to continue without me. Undoubtedly less interesting, but no doubt less cause for anxiety. Oh, horseshit. He will deny he ever supported me. Now, oddly, I am disappointed in that prospect. For no good reason, I'd expected better.

"Then we must follow protocol," he answers, staring above half-glasses. "You must tender your resignation formally, and proceed accordingly."

I agree without issue.

"And I'll organize the farewell party."

I protest.

271

He insists.
I, reluctantly, agree.

77

I decide to wander over to the faculty lounge, to interact with my fellows -- for no good reason other than to show my face and to read what I can in theirs. It is the day before the conference on the teacher as power figure and the lounge is abuzz. While the university has managed to attract a heavy-duty lineup of academicians, psychologists, group dynamicists, et al, I am not all that interested. They will be making presentations that evolve, quickly, into published papers, or are rehashes of previously published papers. Publish or perish. Hmmmmm. Green Cheese. Publish . . . or perish. Publish *and* perish. Anyway, while I enjoy, to a degree, going one-on-one with Angelica Magnus (or rather being punished by her) on the subject, the contest of egos that defines these grand gatherings I find insufferable. The circle jerk of the Pharisees and Philistines. Nor do I really want a part in the preliminaries, don't want to be drawn into the discussion here and now.

Alas.

The Bart v Angelica contest has heated up with Bart unable to cow his less-senior colleague and Angelica unable to force him to concede the strength of her position.

I am content with the sidelines and the occasional unexpressed Olé for the señorita. Despite my own less-than-successful encounters with Angelica, I cannot but root for her against Carpozzi. One cannot help but be impressed by the clarity of her thinking, the build of her argument. Bart is bloody but unbowed. Andy is antsy. I suspect because his cohort will butcher him later for his cowardly silence. Andy, however, will not risk a sortie of

273

his own, so he opts instead for a diversion: "and what do *you* think, Max?"

"Hoomm," I hum from behind my smoke cloud. I consider, briefly, a succession of grunted "nihils," but have done that once before and . . . something is compelling me to play. "It involves the movement away from the pretense of power to the participation of teaching."

"Teaching as a participatory event," Bart chides, "there's a novel concept."

I want to snap back, but I . . . don't want to. "We are a faithless society," I find myself saying in a tone so even-tempered I'm not sure it is coming from me. "We have only the ability to gain and transfer knowledge to keep us in the game. It is the long way around, but it is all we've got." I am beginning to feel a bit warm. They are beginning to stare. "I have only recently come to appreciate my dual nature as teacher/student." Really stare. Something *has* come over me. There is certainly nothing profound in my comments and I await, at any moment, the biting comeback from Bart or . . . Angelica is regarding me with a look that can only be described as reverence. "It's all a matter of convergence, the achievement of unity . . . the . . . I'm sorry," I say, dinching the deadly smoke stick into an ashtray, "I don't feel . . . I'm not sure what has come . . . " I rise, steady my wobbly body against a table, and walk to the door, my view reduced to a blare of white light. I feel I am transiting . . . I can't see anything but the white- white light, but I have no fear that I will find my way to the exit door. I am aware I am there when I feel the fresh air and the blues and greens, and browns and greys return. When I have fully returned to the living, I sense I am the receptor of unshaken attention. I turn to the window of the lounge and they are all there, pressed against the glass,

274

looking like a Flemish painting. I head for my Z and ultimately for Aaley.

78

I am late to my own farewell party; I cannot help it. I don't want to participate in this senseless exercise in protocol, but feel a certain sense of obligation to Simeon for sticking with me -- irrespective of how it advanced, or at least aided, his personal agenda. But now I am making him pay for it a bit by being late and knowing that he is almost to the point of having to explain my absence, interpret my uninterpretable thought patterns, for my supposed colleagues. Fuck 'em. Fuck 'im. When I am out of sight, he'll definitely deny he ever supported me, beyond declaring he tried to usher me away from the errors of my ways.

The elevator opens on the ninth floor of the Student Center and I head in the direction of the loud conversation. At the door to the suite, Bart Carp stands, balancing a scotch-and-water on his forehead and explaining to the female grad student who edits the literary magazine the importance of the physical aspects of one's head. He is so fucking transparent. I consider saying something appropriately provocative. Why bother. When he sees me approach, he exclaims, decidedly drunkenly, "ah, master, entré, mein heir." This is absurd, as are all rituals.

The setting is as I have anticipated. Simeon has done his best to gather the troops, but I know most are simply putting in an appearance in the hopes I will do something more to talk about when I am gone. Cheap wine flows like water. The beer is in cans and lukewarm. I decide upon red wine. It will loosen my tongue; I may as well fulfill the expectations of my colleagues. It is pay-as-you-go. Ah, Simeon, Simeon. I want to ask the bartender

276

if special arrangements have been made for the guest of honor, but know better.

"So, Max," Andy Dagliesh queries (he has crossed the room to reach me -- a man with a mission), "you can make a living writing poetry?"

"Don't be ridiculous," I answer, "I intend to sell crack cocaine."

His eyes widen a shaving. He is just drunk enough to have accepted, for an instant. I am still sober enough to have noticed. The comment silences him; he cannot press, articulate his doubts that I can survive at all in the real world. Now that *is* show-stopping, disconcerting. He wanders off, his repertoire exhausted.

I determine not to circulate, hold my position, make them come to me, pay homage. It doesn't promise much in the way of entertainment, but I know eventually they will gather 'round, then who knows? The possibilities are too seductive. They are all story-tellers; they need nourishment. They will feed upon me.

And the universe rotates.

"Where the hell have you been?" Simeon asks.

"Yes."

He does not skip a beat. "You won't be happy until you drag me down with you, won't you?"

"Yes."

"Yes what?!"

"Sir?"

He grimaces, smirks.

"I've done it," I declare.

"Done what?"

"It."

He's had it, turns to leave.

"The poem."

He turns back. "What about it?"

277

I survey his eyes, then, "nothing," I say. "Nothing."
He departs.

Nihil, the non-word word, the connection. . . . *that which is not cannot in any way be something.*[1] ? Bart Carp with a drink teetering on his forehead. Andy Dagliesh with his informed skepticism about my poetry. Simeon with his angry denial. All rituals. The sound and the fury of idiots signifying . . . The signs. The facilitators of knowledge. The barriers to wisdom. Signifying . . . nothing. Nada. Nix. Niente. Nein. Nine? Three times three. Nihil. Whether you approach through knowledge or faith, you still end up at zero. That which is not cannot in any way be something. Can that which we perceive as something progress to nothing?

"I seek your approbation, Max," Andy Dagliesh launches. I hadn't seen him returning.

"Get oowt," I respond, sardonically. His facial muscles twitter a bit, then sag. "No, really," he answers.

"*My* approbation?"

"I don't feel I can ask for . . . your love."

He is *really* drunk.

"You have it, Andy . . . "

He is owl-eyed.

"My approbation and . . . why not? And my love."

His face tones into an apple-cheeked beatitude.
"Thank you, Max," he puffs.

"Bless you, my son." I can't help myself.

He wobbles off.

"Why Andy?"

I turn abruptly. It is Angelica. Her face is a question mark -- holds.

"His need seemed greatest," I muster.

"And me? . . . And . . . mine?"

"You and yours?"

278

"Yes." And holds.

I release the big breath I now realize I have trapped within. "What is it, Angelica? I'm not sure I see." I fix on her eyes. And I see. I see. Hope. Not hope. A representation of a request for affirmation. "You're frightened."

"Yes.

"And you . . . have never been."

"Out of ignorance."

"Before."

". . . Yes."

She is silent again.

I hunt for words. "A ring-necked pheasant will sniff at your grave."

She breaks almost immediately into a smile. A small smile.

I shake my head and head for the bar. I buy another red wine; swallow it whole. I get still another; determine to go more slowly. A daze is in place quickly, mercifully. The wine, partially. Inadequate blood flow, contributing.

Aaley is in the doorway taking the measure of the surroundings. Simeon notices, heads for her. I don't know that they have ever met, but it is apparent Simeon feels somehow challenged. "May I help you?" he asks her, as I, too, arrive.

"I have come to honor the maestro," she says.

"Only invited guests," he counters.

"She *is* with me," I respond.

He yearns to protest but decides better of it. His role as my interlocutor is threatened. He no longer has leverage with which to bargain. The cunt, after all, is fucking me. Who would you bet on? I am unimpressed by these . . . demonstrations: Simeon ascendant; Andy, Angelica blessed. Aaley . . . here . . . for the finale. The finale.

"Are you all right?" she asks when he has left.

279

"Are you kidding?"

"Take me away from all this."

"Later."

"Now."

"Why?"

"Simeon gives me pause. I am afraid of him. He hates women."[2]

"Simeon? He speaks that way because he enjoys the authoritarian mode. He loves the sound of his own voice. He needs to pontificate."

"He wants to destroy me."

I half-smile, shake my head.

"He hates women."

God, she's beautiful. She *is* the one. "They are jealous of you, all of them. You are what they are not. Free to articulate whatever you happen to be thinking. Free to examine, accept, reject -- change your mind. They are connected to positions they have established. They have written their own histories (and they will write mine, I am sure). They cannot back away without admitting the flaws in their arguments, the weakness of their reasoning. It is that which frightens them, not hatred for women. Angelica is, after all, a women."

"Doctor Magnus hates me most of all."

"Why would you think that?"

"My relationship with you."

The scream! Distant. Across the river. On the far side. Approaching like a wave of warriors. It's been a while since I've had to suffer an all-out assault. I'd forgotten, almost. Now it is pinging then ringing, strung like beads that burrow through my ears.

"You are wide-eyed, white-faced, flat," she says. "Come. Quickly."

She leads me, literally drags me into the men's room. Pulls off my jacket and drops it to the floor, tugs my tie from my collar, unbuttons the top three buttons. "Put your head in the sink," she commands.

My head is the target of a pathologist's bone saw. I'll do anything she says. I drop my face into the wash-bowl. She is fumbling through her purse. Stops. Un-screws a cap. The room fills with ambrosia. Liquid runs over my head, streams behind my ears, across my neck and into the sink. Her fingers work the base of my skull with the dexterity and strength of Terri Sas. I am in a swoon. My brain has been anesthetized. It is heaven.

A toilet flushes. I hear a booth door open and swing closed. A foul smell fights that of the ointment.

"What *is* that aroma?" It is Bart Carp's voice. I wonder to which he refers.

"A special salve," she responds, in an obedient tone.

"It must have cost a fortune."

"He had a deadly headache."

"A couple of aspirins would have done the trick."

"Hey," I say, "What do you give a shit? The treat-ment worked."

"An extravagance," he insists. "Could have fed the ghetto for a week." He stalks out.

As if he gave a shit.

"I need some air," I say.

"Come," she says, "I'll take you to one of those benches on the quad."

We steal away, without further interaction. We find a bench by the tulip garden, where I rejoice in the cool night breeze and the fresh smell of the foliage.

281

79

Children are unfinished business.

80

Today, thou shalt be with me in Paradise.
What about Aaley?
[Blip.]

81

God is showing off.

Somehow, I feel it is for me. The sky is salmon-colored; the landline redbrickbuildings or elevatedtrains. Blueblackclouds sit like dirty pulls of cotton, an arm'slength away, their undersides stringystrands hanging beneath. Have I done something right? The red taillights of escaping autos seem redder than they are. The black silhouette of an imperfect pine seems . . . is perfect. Discarded papers and rusting drums seem not inappropriate. What is going on here? A cleanfresh rain; a warmdry sun.

Ore on ore, clicketyclackety hiss bump clicketyclack whizz. Dewlubed smell of burningsteel. A page, the finalentry on treeplanks by the window. The golden temple against the mountain in the black. I am empty save for the faintremainder of the X, nowandforever. I await the coming stasis, not the contradiction it would seem if I were not emptynearcomplete.

I Tiresias, though blind, throbbing between two lives[1]

The bullet hits me just above the left temple. I don't know how I know this, but I do. The missile has exploded the jellied mass inside my brain and I can no longer think.

Bless me, Father, for I have sinned.

But I am still communicating, so what *is* happening here? Perhaps this is another dream, one of my hallucinations -- but I think not. At least not within the context of reality, as I had come to know it. But I am still communicating, even though my mind has been destroyed. Does that mean I am dead? But I am still on the train. I can still feel it rocking, smell the sharp smell of burning metal. The wheels grinding against the rails wet with morning rain. I can still feel the car jouncing over its imperfect trackbed. I can see now the broadexpanse of marshland. And I am being drawn to it.

I squeeze through the frayed circle where the bullet penetrated the window glass. It looks like a puckered asshole and somehow that seems appropriate. Enter life through a rubbercunt, leave through a glassasshole. I'd long suspected God a comedian and I'm glad to see that in death I have regained *my* senseofhumor. You know, I didn't hear anyone scream or even cry out when the bullet crushed my skull and noone has shouted after me now that I am leaving. I guess noone will miss me

Aa

I head for the swamp. I listen for the shebird. I cannot hear her. I slide down the gravel grade that slopes from the rightofway and I cringe in anticipation of the cinderstonerasping of my legs. But there is none and I knew of course that there wouldnotbe. I slip into the waters of the cattail marsh just beyond the tall fence of the driving range where rich Orientals launch golfballs into the metal mesh like planets caught in a fishnet. But the balls are passing through the net, over my head -- *through* my head -- like liberated quarks dancing through a wall of lead. Three quacks for Muster Max.[2] I don't feel a thing, save the water which is rising about my waist as I muckluck through the swamp toward the deeper waters of the bay. Still, the shebird's silent.

Blow! blow! blow!
Blow up sea-winds along Paumanok's shore:
I wait and I wait till you blow my mate to me.[3]

285

The water is neither cold nor warm. It is a neutrality, but I can feel it, at least I know it is there. I have knowledge of its presence. I am sure of this. Sure. Sum. Cogito ergo sum. Sapio ergo sum. Sum.

I am in a boilingsoup of detritus, trilobites, amphibians, smallmammals, all slithering about. The water of the bay is roiling toward me. Perhaps it is a submarine on its way through my brain. What the fuck. Why not? Everything else seems to be passing through there today. Say,
what day
is today
anyway?
0 day

The doctor is late. The night is blackonwhite. The road is blowingsnow over an inch of ice. At the edge of hervision appears, as if from nowhere, a mother grasping the hand of a child. In the headlights the child freezes, momentarily. The mother jerks her clear of the road, narrowed by the snow packed along its perimeter. At the sametime, the doctor swerves, instinctively, hits the brakes, erroneously, turning the vehicle broadside to its momentum. I can see the fear on the driver's face, the familiarface, before the impact against the tree, a solid beech with characteristically lowslung, trunklike branches, oneofwhich implodes the driver'sside door, killing the loneoccupant with one crushing blow to the heart. Odd, she seems mucholder than I remember. The motherandchild are fine.

I am here and there and hereandthere. And he is there and here and here and there. And then he is gone. I have sensed his presence, I still sense his presence, I will sense his presence. And he is gone. And he has never been, but he will always be. Gone. Alwaysbegone. For he has lost it and I have found it again. I know he has never had it because I haveneverlostit. And the roiling,

286

coiling, undulating vibration neverwas, neveris, never-willbe. And the train is rolling onward, toward the shore. And has not moved an inch. Because the shore has never moved. It is here. It is there. Is everywhere. For the coil that roiled in the linear boil could not comprehend the spiral, which winds ever inward on itself, homing in on the point it cannot reach this time. This time.

Terror is on the breeze, the soft breathbreeze. Can't shake the memory. Have no fear. Come to me. Come.

Eyes wide in fright, terror grips the soft breath-breeze. Still split from me.

Teeth of a bishop are sunk into her forearm, down to the bone.[4] She shakes him loose. A king tears at her skull and runs off with it encased in a reliquary.[4] She doesn't need it anymore. The flesh and bones. Margaret Montgomery is gone. Then fear is dead.

Cometome.

Terror dissipates and with a sigh the breathbreeze dies.

A breeze blows softsandripples across the wetland. The softbreathbreeze. I look yet do not see; search yet find. The breathbreeze not visible yet there. An echo bounces off the walls inside my hollow brain -- *headpiece made of straw*[5] . . . no, clay . . . ceramic. My brainhollow. Not there. No more. The explosion destroyed it. The explosion didn't matter. Matterdidn'tmatter. I am a hollow shell yet filled, perhaps fulfilled. I do not need to see to know. I know. Iknow. I am. You are. Amare.

The spirit leads her. She is here. She is there. She is everywhere. Not that time, this time, any time. And I'm.

She touches my hand. I go in her. Do not move. We connect. My eyes well up in tears; they flow over the lower lids. The nostalgia is real; the experience real. We fuse in water and light. She melds with me and the world

287

begins to close. The leaves are falling all around us, spin-
ning inward in an intensifying wind. She is a wonder of
loveliness. Of lovely... of love. As we couple, I can't even
remember the word. The sightsmellsoundtastetouch of her
is all. A single allconsuming nonsense. Is love...ly. The
corruption is . . . was. My father and mother are. Were.
Somewhere. Are not part of me anymore. Now,
neverwere, willbe. Shewithme, is *sin*sin. Ur-non-ur. Becomes the ur. *Pure of sinful thought. . . she turn's; I follow'd her. . . The earth gave sign of gratulation . . . The
evening star to light the bridal lamp.*[6]

> For I should not have known how to love
> The Lord if He had not loved me. For who
> is able to distinguish love, except the
> one that is loved.[7]

Everything goes white. The light becomes liquid,
amniotic fluid. Then begins the suction to the point, the ex-
purgation of worldly knowledgeand

thereunionwithpureknowledgethatcomeswithfaith.

*I am lifted and carried along the shining coverlet
and set down on the sand.*[8]

I am wrapped in the shroud in the original tomb.
She is wrapped to me.

*Learn your true identity.
Receive your own name.*[9]

He is in the room.

0/1.

Altagracia.

Then, up from the glow of the liquidwhiteflow, a
tinyhand grasps a straw in a steelgrip and transforms it to a
staff of gold.

"Iam theson/daughterofmanbornofwoman," the
voice says, "here to tend mygarden."

He drives the staff into the sodden earth of the salt-marsh. And the earth shudders below. It quivers ripples across the marsh, rattles pebbles on the road, vibrates the walls of the buildings in the community surrounding.

The pages flutter in the breeze on the treeplanks by the window, then blow out and out, then out and back like a greencheese satellite in a gravitational trap. The final page lays on the treeplanks unaffected by the wind, unconcerned with the wind. It sits, the sheet, four words upon:

kindly
disregard
this
poem
•

Notes and References

Chapter 01

1. Walt Whitman, *Leaves of Grass*, "Song of Myself," Stanza 15
2. Emily Dickinson, *Collected Poems*, No. 324
3. Ralph Waldo Emerson, *Essays*
4. Edgar Allan Poe, "Annabel Lee"
5. Gospel of Matthew, 27:46, "Father, Father, why hast thou fore-saken me?"

Chapter 02

1. John Milton, "Paradise Lost," Book VI, Line 829
2. James Joyce, *Finnegans Wake*, "Anna Livia" chapter, ". . . death cap mushrooms round Funglus grave . . ."
3. Reference to "The Love Song of J. Alfred Prufrock," T.S. Eliot, Stanza 6, Line 3: "Time to turn back and descend the stair, / With a bald spot in the middle of my hair --"

Chapter 03

1."Don't touch me." Christ's words to Mary Magdalen when she reaches out to touch him after the Resurrection.
2. Dante, *The Divine Comedy*, "Inferno," Canto III, at the River Acheron
3. Wallace Stevens, *The Palm at the End of the Mind*, "Anecdote of the Jar."

Chapter 03 (cont'd)

4. Paraphrase of lines from "The Love Song of J. Alfred Prufrock," T.S. Eliot.
5. Takeoff on "The Raven," Edgar Allan Poe.
6. Takeoff on "The Love Song of J. Alfred Prufrock."
7. John Milton, "Paradise Lost," Book VI, Line 864

Chapter 05

1. "I am who I am." Old Testament God, Yahweh.

Chapter 08

1. St. Aurelius Augustine, *De magistro*, Chapter II
2. ibid, Chapter XIV
3. ibid
4. Two puppets of a children's television show, "Sesame Street," on the public network. They were teachers of a sort.

Chapter 10

1. Working title of James Joyce's *Finnegans Wake*.
2. Federico García Lorca, *Collected Poems*.
3. Pablo Neruda, *Canto General*.
4. "The afternoon is released on a lyrical green horsewoman," Federico García Lorca, *Collected Poems*.
5. Takeoff on Walt Whitman's "Song of Myself," *Leaves of Grass*.
6. "Body of a Woman," Pablo Neruda, *Canto General*

Chapter 13

1. Emily Dickinson, *Collected Poems*, No. 251
2. *Gospel of Thomas*, Nag Hammadi Library, Jesus speaking.

Chapter 16

1. T.S. Eliot, "Ash Wednesday"
2. ibid

Chapter 18

1. Henry Miller, *Tropic of Cancer*

Chapter 23

1. Emily Dickinson, "A Route of Evanescence"

Chapter 25

1. John Donne, "Air and Angels"
2. ibid

Chapter 27

1. Walt Whitman, *Leaves of Grass*, "Song of Myself," Stanza 6
2. Ralph Waldo Emerson, *Nature*, "VI. Idealism"

Chapter 29

1. Ovid, *Metamorphoses*, Book VI, "Tereus, Procne and Philomela"

Chapter 32

1. John Milton, "When I Consider How My Light is Spent"

Chapter 33

1. James Joyce, *Finnegans Wake*, opening lines

Chapter 35

1. Ovid, Metamorphoses, Book III, "Echo and Narcissus"
2. ibid

Chapter 37

1. Dante, *The Divine Comedy*, "Inferno," Canto IX, the angel opens the gates to the city of Dis.
2. Edgar Allan Poe, "Ulalame"
Note on this chapter: According to *Pistis Sophia*, a Gnostic Gospel, ingestion of a soup of menstrual blood and sperm was part of a mysterious ceremony and designated by Jesus as the greatest of sins.

Chapter 38

1. T.S. Eliot, "The Wasteland"

Chapter 39

1. Hypostasis of the Archons
2. Homer, *The Odyssey*, Book IX, Lines 146-7
3. Hypostasis of the Archons

Chapter 41

1. *Gospel of Thomas,* 46:30-33
2. John Milton, "Paradise Lost," Book VIII, Lines 437-448

Chapter 41 (cont'd)

3. Sir Thomas Browne, *Religio Medici*
4. Book of Job, 10:15

Chapter 43

1. Jesus speaking, *Gospel of Thomas* 37:34

Chapter 45

1. Takeoff on Isaiah, Chapters 40-42.

Chapter 46

1. Random selections from John Milton, "Paradise Lost," "Paradise Regained."

Chapter 49

1. T.S. Eliot, "Ash Wednesday"
2. Pope Clement re perversity, *The Acts of John*, Nag Hammadi Library

Chapter 51

1. Tiresias to Creon, Sophocles, *Antigone*

Chapter 53

1. Ezra Pound considered to the process of creating a poem as sculpting a block of air
2. T.S. Eliot refers to Pound as miglior fabbro -- "the better craftsman" -- in the epigram to "The Wasteland."